PANAMA

COSTA RICA

VENEZUELA

GUYANA

SURINAME

FRENCH GUIANA

COLOMBIA

ECUADOR

Equator

AMAZONIA

BRAZIL

EAST BRAZIL

PERU

ANDES

BOLIVIA

ANDES
MOUNTAINS

PARAGUAY

GRAN
CHACO

CHILE

ARGENTINA

URUGUAY

SOUTHERN
SOUTH
AMERICA

Pacific Ocean

Atlantic Ocean

These Chipewyans were
photographed about 1917 near
Great Slave Lake, Canada.

REFERENCE

RAND McNALLY
CHILDREN'S ATLAS OF

NATIVE AMERICANS

RAND McNALLY

CHICAGO   NEW YORK   SAN FRANCISCO

RAND McNALLY
CHILDREN'S ATLAS OF
NATIVE AMERICANS

General Manager: Russell L. Voisin
Managing Editor: Jon M. Leverenz
Editor: Elizabeth Fagan Adelman
Writer: Francis Reddy
Art Director: John Nelson
Designer: James Buddenbaum
Illustrator: David Cunningham
Production Editor: Laura C. Schmidt
Manufacturing Planner: Marianne Abraham

Library of Congress Cataloging-in-Publication Data

Rand McNally & Company.

   Children's Atlas of Native Americans / Rand McNally.
      p. cm.
   Includes index.
   Summary: Maps, illustrations, photographs, and text present the world of North, Central, and South American Indians as they existed a hundred years ago.
      ISBN: 0-528-83494-0
      1 Indians—Juvenile literature. 2. Indians—Maps—Juvenile literature.
   [1. Indians—Maps.] I. Title

   E58.4.R36   1992
   970.004'97—dc20   92-6791
                                                                   CIP
                                                                    AC

Photo Credits
Page 4 Chipewyan: National Museum of the American Indian, Smithsonian Institution. 8-9 New Mexico: John R. Running. Brazil: National Museum of the American Indian, Smithsonian Institution. 12-13 New Mexico: Mark Nohl, New Mexico Economic & Tourism Dept. 14-15 Ohio: Ohio Historical Society. 16-17 Chichén Itzá: Francis Reddy. Teotihuacán: Robert Frerck/Odyssey Prod./Chicago. Xochicalco: Milwaukee Public Museum. 18-19 Guatemala: Robert Frerck/Odyssey Prod./Chicago. Mexico: Robert Frerck/Odyssey Prod./Chicago. 20-21 Sacsahuaman: Robert Frerck/Odyssey Prod./Chicago. Tambo Machay: Robert Frerck/Odyssey Prod./Chicago. Machu Picchu: Robert Frerck/Odyssey Prod./Chicago. 24-25 Eskimo: Milwaukee Public Museum. 28-29 Kutchin: National Museum of the American Indian, Smithsonian Institution. 30-31 Kwakiutl: Milwaukee Public Museum. 32-33 Haida: National Anthropological Archives, Smithsonian Institution. Tlingit: National Anthropological Archives, Smithsonian Institution. 36-37 Powhatan: National Museum of the American Indian, Smithsonian Institution. Massachuset: National Museum of the American Indian, Smithsonian Institution. 40-41 Mohawk: National Anthropological Archives, Smithsonian Institution. Menominee: Milwaukee Public Museum. 42-43 Seminole: National Museum of the American Indian, Smithsonian Institution. 44-45 Cherokee: National Anthropological Archives, Smithsonian Institution. Creek: National Museum of the American Indian, Smithsonian Institution. 48-49 Hidatsa: Milwaukee Public Museum. 50-51 Mandan: Milwaukee Public Museum. Arapaho: National Anthropological Archives, Smithsonian Institution. Blackfoot: National Anthropological Archives, Smithsonian Institution. 54-55 Shoshoni: National Anthropological Archives, Smithsonian Institution. Ute: National Anthropological Archives, Smithsonian Institution. Paiute: National Anthropological Archives, Smithsonian Institution. 56-57 Klamath: National Museum of the American Indian, Smithsonian Institution. 60-61 Navajo: Arizona Office of Tourism. 62-63 Two Apache: National Anthropological Archives, Smithsonian Institution. Hopi: Milwaukee Public Museum. 64-65 Zapotec site: Milwaukee Public Museum. Zapotec women: National Museum of the American Indian, Smithsonian Institution. 72-73 Mapuche: National Museum of the American Indian, Smithsonian Institution. Araucanian: National Anthropological Archives, Smithsonian Institution.

 Printed on recycled paper.

CONTENTS

INTRODUCTION

Indians were the first human inhabitants of the Americas. The buildings of Pueblo Bonito at Chaco Canyon, New Mexico, held 800 rooms in apartments up to five stories high. Anasazi Indians first occupied the site around AD 900.

Most people picture the horse-riding buffalo hunters of the Great Plains when they think of American Indians. Yet this life-style did not develop until the late 1700s, long after the arrival of Europeans and their horses. Shown here is a Plains Indian community.

It is believed that centuries before prehistoric cave paintings were created by humans in what is now France, ancestors of modern American Indians crossed the Bering Land Bridge into North America. Over thousands of years, they spread throughout the land, their life-styles varying with the environments they encountered. As many as 100 million people representing some 2,000 different cultures inhabited the Americas at the time of European contact around the year 1500. Today, descendants of these people are known as Native Americans or American Indians.

Some groups hunted animals and gathered plants for food, but other groups grew their own foods. Many of the plants native farmers cultivated, such as corn, beans, potatoes, tomatoes, and squashes, existed nowhere else and today represent important foods throughout the world.

This atlas is an introduction to the diverse native cultures that once occupied all of North, Central, and South America. In general, the maps show the area occupied by native groups when they were most widespread, before the arrival of large numbers of Europeans in the 1500s. But it is important to remember that Native Americans are not merely part of the past. They are people that live today, and their cultures and traditions are still alive. It is important for everyone to honor and help preserve their ancient heritage.

Indian cultures spread throughout the Americas. The different environments shaped the Indians' life-styles. These are Indians of the Amazon rain forest in South America.

BERING LAND BRIDGE APPROXIMATE
SHORELINE 18,000 YEARS AGO

GREENLAND

Arctic Circle

Nome•

UNITED STATES
(AK)

■ BLUEFISH CAVES, CANADA
25,000 YEARS AGO?

*Hudson
Bay*

C A N A D A

ROCKY MOUNTAINS

Great Lakes

APPALACHIAN MTS.

•Boston

MEADOWCROFT ROCKSHELTER, U.S.
19,600 YEARS AGO?

U N I T E D
S T A T E S

Atlantic Ocean

Los Angeles •

■ CLOVIS, U.S.
11,000 YEARS AGO

SIERRA MADRE

Gulf of Mexico

M E X I C O

Pacific Ocean

Mexico City•

CUBA

Caribbean Sea

BELIZE
HONDURAS
GUATEMALA   NICARAGUA
EL SALVADOR
                PANAMA
            COSTA RICA

■ TAIMA-TAIMA, VENEZUELA
13,000 YEARS AGO?

VENEZUELA

SURINAME

GUYANA

FRENCH
GUIANA

Santa Fe
de Bogotá

COLOMBIA

Equator

ECUADOR

B R A Z I L

PERU

ANDES MOUNTAINS

GUITARRERO CAVE, PERU
12,000 YEARS AGO

• Rio de Janiero
• São Paulo

BOLIVIA

PARAGUAY

This large map shows the probable
routes early humans took when they
crossed the Bering Land Bridge.
Archeological sites and approximate dates during which they were
occupied are shown. The small,
round map shows what this area
looks like on the planet earth.

Pacific Ocean

TAGUA TAGUA, CHILE
11,400 YEARS

Santiago•

CHILE

URUGUAY

• Buenos Aires

ARGENTINA

Atlantic Ocean

MONTE VERDE, CHILE
13,000 YEARS AGO?

0   500   1000 Mi.
0   500 1000 Km.
Scale

10

ORIGINS

THE FIRST AMERICANS

Humans discovered America during the last Ice Age, when vast sheets of ice covered about one-third of the earth's surface. The ice locked away huge amounts of ocean water, reducing the sea level by more than 300 feet (91.4 meters). Where the Bering Strait now separates Asia and North America, the low sea level exposed a bridge of land that linked the two continents. Between thirty thousand and fifty thousand years ago, small bands of nomadic Asians crossed this land bridge and entered North America.

They came in waves of small groups over thousands of years, gradually spreading throughout the continent. These first Americans probably followed migrating herds of now-extinct animals, which they depended on for food. By 20,000 BC, nomadic hunters had spread throughout North America. They continued expanding southward, reaching the tip of South America by 10,000 BC.

They lived in small groups in caves or under wooden shelters, and used fire for cooking and protection. They clothed themselves in animal hides and furs. They hunted the big game of the vast grasslands and also gathered seeds, berries, and roots.

Their tools were made of stone and bone. Their spear points date from between 10,000 BC to 7000 BC and can be found throughout the contiguous United States, Alaska, southern Canada, and northern Mexico.

Following herds of migrating animals, nomadic tribes crossed the land bridge between Asia and North America during the last Ice Age. The Americas were the last continents to be occupied by humans.

The ancient cliffside homes of the Rio Grande Anasazi now stand in ruin at Bandelier National Monument, New Mexico. A group of Anasazi inhabited these dwellings from about AD 1400 to the late 1500s.

CLIFF DWELLERS AND MOUND BUILDERS

Between 10,000 and 5000 BC, the climate warmed, and the vast glaciers and ice sheets retreated northward. The big game upon which early American Indians depended became extinct, both because of the changing climate and overhunting. Native Americans now hunted and trapped small animals, and fish and wild plants played a more important role in their diet. They developed new tools and used a wider variety of materials, including wood, antler, and ivory. They learned how to store and preserve food, weave plant fibers into clothing and baskets, and build boats.

Now that American Indians no longer tracked the movements of great herds, they wandered less and less. They began cultivating plants instead of simply collecting them. American farming began in Mexico, but some knowledge had filtered north into what is now the southwestern United States by about 3500 BC. With the development of a stable food supply, Native American cultures became more organized. From about 300 BC to AD 1300, three early desert cultures shaped life in the Southwest—the Mogollon, the Hohokam, and the Anasazi.

The Mogollon (southwestern New Mexico) and Hohokam (southeastern Arizona) people farmed mountain valleys to grow tobacco, cotton, corn, beans, and squash. They lived in underground dwellings called "pit houses," using the earth to protect themselves from the temperature extremes of the desert. The Mogollon are thought to be the first Southwest people to build houses, farm, and make pottery. The Hohokam developed an irrigation system, digging

Bering Sea

UNITED STATES
(AK)

● Anchorage

Yukon *River*

Mackenzie River

Great Bear Lake

Great Slave Lake

Arctic Circle

Hudson Bay

C A N A D A

Lake Winnipeg

● Calgary

Seattle ●

River

Columbia

Missouri River

Great

Lakes

Montréal ●

APPALACHIAN MOUNTAINS

New York ●

Atlantic Ocean

R O C K Y   M O U N T A I N S

Great Salt Lake

U N I T E D   S T A T E S

Mississippi

□ AZTALAN, WI

Chicago ●

CHILLICOTHE, OH □   □ MOUNDSVILLE, WV

CAHOKIA, IL ⊡

GREAT SERPENT
MOUND, OH ⊡

Ohio

River

This map shows some of the better-
known sites of the cliff-dwelling
Anasazi ■ and the mound-building
Adena □ and Mississippian ⊡
peoples. Many of these sites are
open to visitors today.

San Francisco ●

River

Colorado

■ MESA VERDE, CO

CANYON DE
CHELLY, AZ ■   ■ CHACO
CANYON, NM

Los Angeles ●

⊡ ETOWAH, GA

SPIRO, OK ⊡

OCMULGEE, GA ⊡

cific Ocean

Dallas ●

BELCHER, LA ⊡

River

MOUNDVILLE, AL ⊡

SIERRA MADRE

Rio

Grande

Miami ●

Gulf of Mexico

CUBA

M E X I C O

Guadalajara ●

Mexico City ●

BELIZE

HONDURAS

GUATEMALA

EL SALVADOR

NICARAGUA

Caribbean Sea

0   400   800 Mi.

0   400   800 Km.

Scale

canals as long as 10 miles (16 kilometers) to help them water their desert crops.

The Anasazi spread throughout the Southwest. They developed a new form of architecture after about AD 750, constructing stone "apartment" dwellings—*pueblos*—on the tops of mesas. They used bricks made from sun-dried mud and straw, called adobe, or built with stones and used adobe to fill in the gaps. After AD 1000, they began building these villages on the ledges of cliffs, which provided better protection against invaders.

These cliff-dwellers used irrigation to increase the production of their farms, and their villages supported large populations. They were excellent builders and artists, creating elaborate pottery, jewelry, and clothing. Severe drought, depletion of the wood supply, and invading tribes probably caused the Anasazi to retreat to smaller settlements around AD 1300.

Three other early Indian cultures appeared in eastern and central North America: the Adena (1000 BC to AD 200), the Hopewell (300 BC to AD 700), and the Mississippian (AD 700 to 1500). They built tens of thousands of earthen *mounds*, primarily in the Mississippi and Ohio river valleys. The mounds of the Adena and Hopewell cultures were used mostly for the burial of their leaders, but a few nonburial mounds in symbolic shapes also appeared.

Mounds took on an additional purpose for the later Mississippian Indians, who used them as the platforms for temples and other important buildings. Their large-scale farming methods supported enormous populations. The Cahokia site in Illinois, the largest Mississippian center, held nearly one hundred burial and temple mounds and a population of tens of thousands.

Monk's Mound rises 100 feet (30.5 meters) above central Cahokia, a vast Mississippian center in Illinois. The city sprawled over 4,000 acres (1,620 hectares) and was built between AD 700 and 1500.

A walkway surrounds the Great Serpent Mound, a 1,330-foot (405-meter) Adena culture earthwork near Peebles, Ohio.

THE GREAT CIVILIZATIONS

America's most complex early civilizations arose to the south, in central and southern Mexico and along the west coast of South America. The earliest of these groups was the *Maya*, whose civilization spread throughout the lands we now know as Guatemala, Honduras, Belize, and southern Mexico.

The Maya and other native groups of this region cultivated over a hundred different types of plants, and this plentiful food supply supported large populations throughout the area for thousands of years. After about 900 BC, the Maya began intensive farming activities, digging hundreds of miles of canals to drain and water their fields. Maya farmers asked for forgiveness before clearing the land. "Oh god," they would pray, "be patient with me. I must ask

Between AD 1 and 150, the people of the city of Teotihuacán built the enormous Pyramid of the Sun, shown here at the upper left.

This Mayan observatory, built around AD 900, stands in the heart of Chichén Itzá, Mexico. Later buildings, such as the pyramid in the background, show the influence of Toltec invaders.

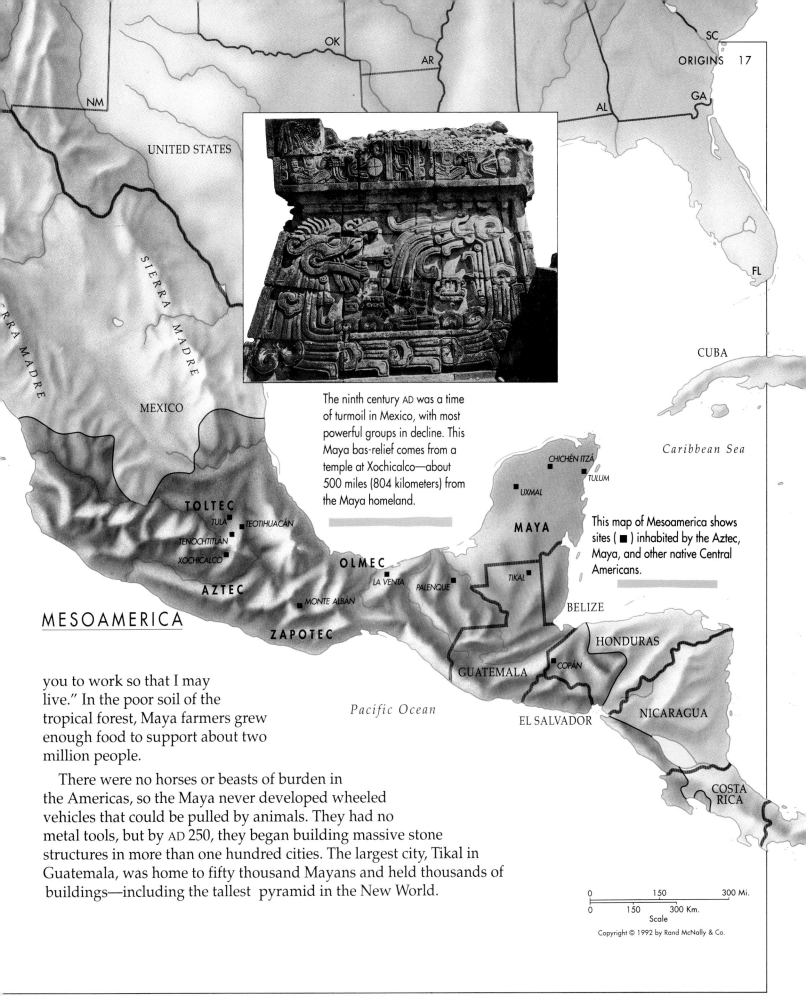

OK

AR

SC

GA

AL

NM

UNITED STATES

FL

CUBA

SIERRA MADRE

RRA MADRE

Caribbean Sea

MEXICO

CHICHÉN ITZÁ

TULUM

The ninth century AD was a time of turmoil in Mexico, with most powerful groups in decline. This Maya bas-relief comes from a temple at Xochicalco—about 500 miles (804 kilometers) from the Maya homeland.

UXMAL

MAYA

TOLTEC

This map of Mesoamerica shows sites (■) inhabited by the Aztec, Maya, and other native Central Americans.

TULA

TEOTIHUACÁN

TENOCHTITLÁN

OLMEC

XOCHICALCO

LA VENTA

PALENQUE

TIKAL

AZTEC

MONTE ALBÁN

BELIZE

MESOAMERICA

ZAPOTEC

HONDURAS

GUATEMALA

COPÁN

you to work so that I may live." In the poor soil of the tropical forest, Maya farmers grew enough food to support about two million people.

Pacific Ocean

NICARAGUA

EL SALVADOR

There were no horses or beasts of burden in the Americas, so the Maya never developed wheeled vehicles that could be pulled by animals. They had no metal tools, but by AD 250, they began building massive stone structures in more than one hundred cities. The largest city, Tikal in Guatemala, was home to fifty thousand Mayans and held thousands of buildings—including the tallest pyramid in the New World.

COSTA RICA

0   150   300 Mi.

0   150   300 Km.

Scale

From the tropical forest along a mountain ridge in present-day Guatemala, the Maya built the city of Tikal. The major temples shown here were built around AD 700.

Master astronomers and mathematicians, the Maya gave their calendar an accuracy not matched in Europe until 1582. They advanced an ancient picture-based form of writing and became the first New World group to keep written records. Maya culture declined around AD 1200, although a few coastal trading towns survived for several hundred years more.

People calling themselves the *Mexicas* arrived in central Mexico around 1200. Forced to compete with neighboring groups for the good farmland, they built their first villages in 1325 on land no one else wanted—the swampy islands within Lake Texcoco. We know these people as *Aztecs*, after their legendary homeland of Aztlan.

They dug canals to drain the swamp and created new farmland by making artificial islands. The main village of Tenochtitlán grew, expanding outward on this new land. Canals connected its thousands of stone buildings. The city had parks, a zoo, aqueducts that brought fresh water into the city from the mainland, and a population of some two hundred thousand. Like the Mayans and other groups of this area, the Aztecs used chocolate beans as a form of money—and a chocolate drink was the preferred beverage of the ruling class. Tenochtitlán, one of the world's largest cities in its day, stood where Mexico City now stands.

Helped by neighboring cities, Tenochtitlán ruled the Valley of Mexico by 1431. The Aztecs then began expanding their empire, conquering neighboring towns and forcing them to pay taxes in the

An Aztec temple, probably built between AD 1300 and 1470, is excavated in the shadows of modern structures in present-day Mexico City.

The warrior Toltecs were the most powerful people in Mexico between AD 900 and 1250. The ruins of their capital, Tula, are about 50 miles (80 kilometers) northwest of Mexico City.

form of food or in raw materials like gold, silver, copper, and jade. Conquest also furnished the Aztecs with war captives for sacrifice to their gods, a part of their religion shared with older groups such as the Maya and the Toltecs. The Aztec Empire stretched from the Atlantic to the Pacific coasts, but it was held together by force and many cities were eager for revolt. People unhappy with Aztec rule assisted the army of Spanish adventurer Hernán Cortés, and in 1521 Tenochtitlán and the Aztec Empire fell.

The mountain fortress of Machu Picchu was probably the last Inca stronghold after the Spanish conquest of Peru in the 1500s. It was not discovered by whites until 1911.

The Incas of South America developed the New World's most organized and widespread culture. Their origins are unclear, but by AD 1100 they dominated the Cuzco valley in what is now Peru. After 1438 they began a rapid expansion of their territory, crushing neighboring groups with their mighty army. Just before the arrival of Europeans, the Inca Empire stretched 2,500 miles (over 4,000 kilometers) along the Pacific coast of South America, from present-day Ecuador to northwestern Argentina.

To help them keep this vast empire together, the Inca built 12,000 miles (19,000 kilometers) of roads. The roads were for llamas, which could carry small loads, and people. Although the Inca did not develop a written language, the *quipu*—knotted strings serving as a memory aid for counting—stored the numerous records of Inca surveys and population counts.

The Inca converted the steep slopes of highland valleys into terraced farmland, complete with irrigation systems. They built elaborate stone structures and created beautiful tapestries, pottery, and metalwork. The sun god was the central figure of Inca religion. Upon the death of the last Inca ruler, Huayna Capac, in 1527, his sons fought for control and plunged the empire into civil war. The war ended in 1532, but the weakened empire proved unable to resist a new challenge—the Spanish conquest of Peru led by Francisco Pizarro.

Shown here is Sacsahuaman, another Inca stronghold, built high in the towering Andes Mountains near Cuzco, Peru.

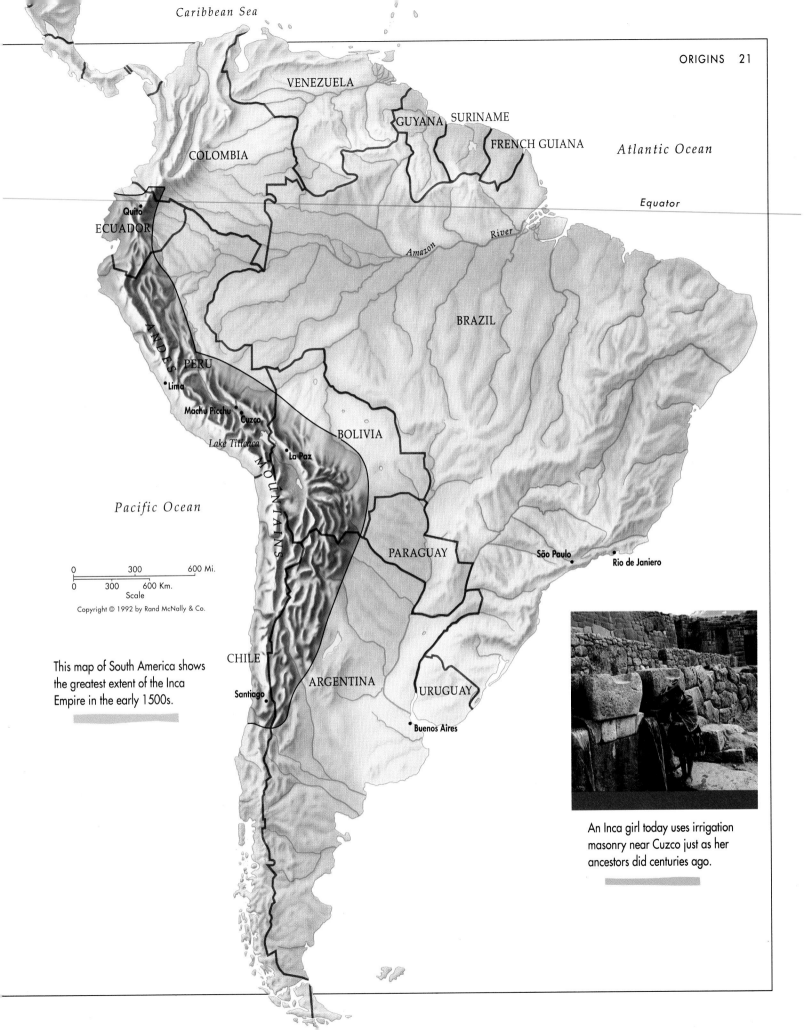

Caribbean Sea

VENEZUELA

GUYANA SURINAME

COLOMBIA

FRENCH GUIANA

Atlantic Ocean

Quito•

ECUADOR

Equator

River

Amazon

BRAZIL

ANDES

PERU

•Lima

Machu Picchu•

Cuzco•

Lake Titicaca

BOLIVIA

•La Paz

Pacific Ocean

M O U N T A I N S

São Paulo•

Rio de Janiero•

PARAGUAY

0   300   600 Mi.

0   300   600 Km.
Scale

Copyright © 1992 by Rand McNally & Co.

CHILE

URUGUAY

This map of South America shows
the greatest extent of the Inca
Empire in the early 1500s.

ARGENTINA

Santiago•

Buenos Aires•

An Inca girl today uses irrigation
masonry near Cuzco just as her
ancestors did centuries ago.

GREENLAND

Bering
Sea

Nome

Aleutian
Islands

Yukon River

UNITED STATES
(AK)

Anchorage

Arctic Circle

ARCTIC

Mackenzie River

Great Bear Lake

Great Slave Lake

SUBARCTIC

Hudson Bay

NORTHWEST
COAST

CANADA

Calgary

Lake Winnipeg

Montréal

Seattle

Columbia River

ROCKY   MOUNTAINS

Missouri River

Mississippi

Great Lakes

APPALACHIAN MOUNTAINS

New York

Great Salt
Lake

UNITED   STATES

Chicago

Ohio River

San Francisco

Colorado River

Atlantic
Ocean

Los Angeles

Pacific Ocean

Dallas

River

SIERRA MADRE

Rio Grande

Gulf of Mexico

Miami

The large map shows the northern-
most culture regions of North
America. The small, round map
shows approximately the same
area on the planet earth.

MEXICO

CUBA

Guadalajara

Mexico City

BELIZE

Caribbean Se

GUATEMALA

HONDURAS

0   400   800 Mi.

0   400   800 Km.

EL SALVADOR

NICARAGUA

Scale

PEOPLES OF THE NORTH

ESKIMO AND ALEUT

Geographic areas within which native groups share similar language and life-style are sometimes called "culture areas." The Eskimo, or Inuit, and Aleut peoples live in the Arctic culture area, which extends more than 5,000 miles (over 8,000 kilometers) across northern Alaska and Canada and even includes parts of Siberia and Greenland. In fact, the Arctic culture area is the largest continuous stretch of land occupied by any group of common cultures on earth.

Ancestors of the Eskimo and Aleut reached North America much later than other Native Americans. They probably arrived by boat between 3000 and 1000 BC, long after the land bridge across the Bering Strait had disappeared.

Like many American Indian groups, Eskimos call themselves a name that translates into English roughly as "the people." That name is "Inuit." "Eskimo" is a name the neighboring Algonquian-speaking people called the Inuit.

The Eskimo included many groups of people with different life-styles who share a common ancestry and language. They lived in all kinds of dwellings, including huts, hide tents, and igloos. The igloo, a temporary

Armed with harpoons, Eskimo hunters prepare to strike at a large whale from their *umiak*. Fashioned from driftwood and animal hides, these boats were up to 40 feet (12 meters) long.

dwelling built from snow and blocks of ice, was used only in the winter by the Canadian Inuit; in the summer they built tents out of driftwood and animal hides. The Inuit of Alaska and Greenland lived in more permanent structures, building huts from logs, whale ribs, stone, earth, and other available materials.

The Arctic is a harsh land of snow and ice with long, cold winters and short, cool summers. The ground itself never thaws completely, remaining frozen all year in a state called *permafrost*. Trees are unable to grow, and only mosses, lichens, and a few flowering plants thrive. To survive in a region with so little edible vegetation, Arctic people had to become skilled hunters.

Most Inuit groups lived along the shores of Hudson Bay and the Pacific, Arctic, and Atlantic oceans. Fish and sea mammals such as seals, sea lions, walruses, and whales were important sources of food. The *kayak*, a one-person hunting vessel covered with the skin of seals or caribou, enabled hunters to glide silently through the water and sneak up on prey. A much larger boat was used along the Alaskan coast to hunt large whales.

The Inuit also hunted land mammals such as caribou, polar bears, and wolves. They sped across the frozen landscape in sleds pulled by dogs. Other groups used snowshoes or spiked boots to make their way in snow and ice.

Aleut homes, called *barabaras*, were permanent dwellings that often held several families. A hole in the roof let smoke escape, but it also often served as the door.

The Aleut, who occupied the Alaskan peninsula and nearby islands, lived similarly to the Inuit. They lived in houses made of driftwood, whale bone, and earth. They depended on the sea, and using kayak-like boats, traded both with the Inuit and the Indians of the Northwest.

ALEU

Aleutia Islands

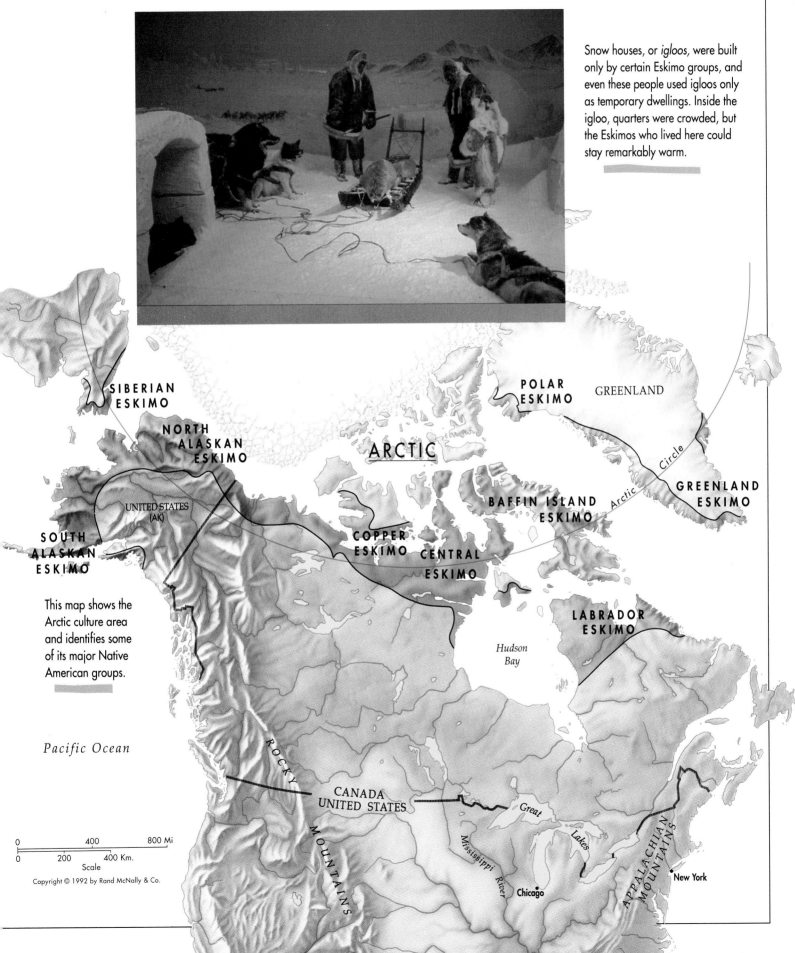

Snow houses, or *igloos*, were built only by certain Eskimo groups, and even these people used igloos only as temporary dwellings. Inside the igloo, quarters were crowded, but the Eskimos who lived here could stay remarkably warm.

SIBERIAN ESKIMO

POLAR ESKIMO

GREENLAND

NORTH ALASKAN ESKIMO

ARCTIC

UNITED STATES (AK)

Arctic Circle

GREENLAND ESKIMO

BAFFIN ISLAND ESKIMO

SOUTH ALASKAN ESKIMO

COPPER ESKIMO

CENTRAL ESKIMO

This map shows the Arctic culture area and identifies some of its major Native American groups.

LABRADOR ESKIMO

Hudson Bay

Pacific Ocean

ROCKY MOUNTAINS

CANADA
UNITED STATES

Great Lakes

APPALACHIAN MOUNTAINS

Mississippi River

New York

Chicago

0   400   800 Mi
0   200   400 Km.
Scale

Copyright © 1992 by Rand McNally & Co.

Aleutian Islands

KUTCHIN, CHIPEWYAN, AND CREE

Heavy summer rains and deep winter snows are typical in the region south of the Arctic. Here in the Subarctic culture area, the pine, spruce, and fir trees of the northern forest struggle to grow in shallow soil. The glaciers that once covered this region left behind lakes, rivers, and swamplands that create seemingly endless waterways. In fact, this area, which includes most of the Alaskan and Canadian interior, holds more than one-seventh of the world's fresh water.

Many American Indian groups occupied the Subarctic, and scholars divide them into two major groups by the languages they spoke. Those living west of Hudson Bay, such as the Kutchin, Chipewyan, and Carrier, spoke Athapascan, while those to the south and east of the bay, like the Cree and Naskapi, spoke the Algonquian language.

Subarctic Indians were hunter-gatherers—they obtained most of their food either by hunting or by gathering the edible plants that grew in the region. Neither the cold, damp climate nor the rocky soil could support farming. These Indians lived in small, mobile groups that usually fished during the summer and hunted during the winter. Migrating herds of caribou

The wanderings and fur-trapping of the Cree of the Subarctic often brought them into conflict with other Native American groups. Cree trappers traded their furs for French and English goods, like beads, cloth, and guns.

GREENLAND

UNITED STATES (AK)

KOYUKON

TANAINA

KUTCHIN

Arctic *Circle*

TUTCHONE

YELLOWKNIFE

DOGRIB

KASKA

CHIPEWYAN

Hudson Bay

BEAVER

SUBARCTIC

CARRIER

CREE

NASKAPI

CREE

CREE

BEOTHUK

ROCKY

CREE

MONTAGNAIS

CANADA
UNITED STATES

OJIBWA

Great

Lakes

Mississippi

M
O
U
N
T
A
I
N
S

Chicago•

• New York

River

A
P
P
A
L
A
C
H
I
A
N

M
O
U
N
T
A
I
N
S

Los Angeles •

This map shows the Subarctic culture area and identifies some of its major American Indian groups.

MEXICO

Atlantic Ocean

Pacific Ocean

Gulf of Mexico

0   400   800 Mi.

0   200   400 Km.

Scale

Copyright © 1992 by Rand McNally & Co.

provided an important source of food and clothing; moose, mountain sheep, and waterfowl were also commonly hunted.

The Kutchin lived in the extreme northwest, on the present-day border of Alaska and Canada. Many Kutchin bands were influenced by the nearby Inuit culture. For example, their flat-bottomed birchbark canoes resembled the Inuit umiak. The Kutchin used narrow snowshoes as long as 6 feet (1.8 meters) to trudge through deep winter snows. They also traveled in Inuit-style sleds rather than the toboggan more commonly used by other Subarctic groups. They built portable cone-shaped dwellings from a wooden framework covered with caribou hides—

These Kutchin children were photographed in Alaska in about 1926, after the Kutchin had given up many of their traditional ways.

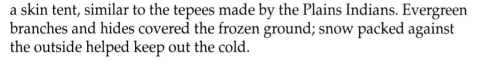

The caribou was a major resource for the Chipewyan. The animal hides were tanned to make tents or clothing, its bones were made into tools, and its meat fed the tribe.

a skin tent, similar to the tepees made by the Plains Indians. Evergreen branches and hides covered the frozen ground; snow packed against the outside helped keep out the cold.

The Chipewyans were the largest Native American group in northwestern Canada and Alaska. They relied heavily on the caribou herds, snaring the animals with ropes, hunting them from bark-covered canoes as they waded across rivers, or herding them into corrals. They used every part of the animal. Its hide was used for clothes, laces, or tent coverings; its bones and antlers became tools. Fish were plentiful throughout the many Subarctic waterways, and Chipewyans caught them any way they could—fish were speared, hooked, or trapped in pens. Chipewyans also ate some of the few plants that grew in this harsh region, such as mosses and lichens.

The widespread Cree were also hunters and trappers. They lived in cone-shaped tents covered with birch bark, or *wigwams*, and traveled by snowshoe or dogsled in winter and by birchbark canoe in summer. They originally lived near Hudson Bay, but by 1650 began a series of migrations that spread them throughout much of Canada. With the arrival of French and English traders in the 1600s, the Cree became a major supplier of animal furs, especially beaver.

One group, the Plains Cree, moved south into the plains of what is now Saskatchewan and Alberta. They took on the life-style of the bison-hunting Plains Indians.

HAIDA, TLINGIT, AND KWAKIUTL

Along the northern Pacific coast of Canada and the United States, ocean currents and offshore winds warm a narrow strip of land that runs 2,000 miles (3,200 kilometers) from what is now California to southern Alaska. Rugged mountains slope down to the ocean and squeeze the moisture out of the sea air, giving this area plenty of rain. The mild climate and great rainfall support the growth of thick forests of fir, spruce, and cedar trees. This is the land of the Northwest Coast culture region.

On islands off the coast of present-day British Columbia lived the Haida. The dense forests provided a rich natural resource, and the Haida were among the most skilled woodworkers of the region. They built large houses from planks of red cedar with beautifully carved *totem poles* towering in front, facing the sea. The entrance to the houses was often a passageway carved in the base of a large totem pole. The figures carved in a totem pole could represent people, animals, or some natural phenomenon that had a special place in the history or legends of each group.

Shown here is an exhibit depicting a Kwakiutl Hamatsa Ceremony. A novice enters a secret room, and a secret society, and is introduced to the heritage of the group's spiritual ancestors. Here the novice is being helped out of the secret room.

UNITED STATES
(AK)

*Aleutian
Islands*

Pacific Ocean

This map shows the Northwest
Coast culture area and identifies
some of its major Native American
groups.

EYAK

Juneau

TLINGIT

NORTHWEST COAST

HAIDA

TSIMSHIAN

BELLA COOLA

BELLA BELLA

ROCKY MOUNTAINS

Vancouver Island   KWAKIUTL

COMOX

NOOTKA

COWICHAN
WA

MAKAH CHEMAKUM   ID   MT   CANADA
Seattle   UNITED STATES

CHINOOK

COWLITZ
OR
Portland

KALAPUYA   WY

COOS

CA

NV

UT

CO

Arctic Circle

0   150   300 Mi.
0   150   300 Km.
Scale

Copyright © 1992 by Rand McNally & Co.

Haida craftsmen also made huge dugout boats from redwood or cedar logs. These boats could be up to 60 feet (18 meters) long and hold dozens of warriors. According to some stories, these canoes carried the Haida as far as Hawaii. Other tribes in the region valued Haida boats, and owning one was a sign of wealth.

The sea was the primary food source for Northwest Coast tribes. Fish were an important part of the Haida diet—particularly halibut, black cod, and salmon—and other seafood included shellfish and sea mammals, such as sea lions and seals.

The Tlingit consisted of thirteen independent bands that occupied the southernmost portions of Alaska. Among the best known were the Auk, Chilkat, and Yakutat. The Tlingit were the great traders of the north. Not only did they trade with other Northwest tribes, but their contacts extended to some Arctic and Subarctic peoples.

The Tlingit shared many traditions with the Haida and other Northwest Coast tribes. They built multifamily cedar houses, carved totem poles, made dugout canoes, and they practiced the complex ceremonies known as *potlatches*. A potlatch could have been part of

These Tlingit men congregated at a potlatch in Alaska in 1901.

different feasts and dances. A household may have given a potlatch at important events, such as the birth, marriage, or death of family members. But it usually served to establish prestige and rank within the village. Those giving a potlatch provided a feast for their guests, and then proceeded to give away or destroy many of their possessions.

Along the shore and islands of southern British Columbia lived the various bands of the Kwakiutl. They were well known for the wooden masks they carved and painted for use in special rituals. Kwakiutl ceremonies were the most elaborate of the area. In the Hamatsa Dance, for example, members of a powerful group took on the roles of spirits, such as Grizzly Bear or Raven, and pretended to perform various acts. This was followed by a potlatch exchange. Because of the work of anthropologists in the 1800s, the life-style of the Kwakiutl is among the best documented of all Native American cultures.

Totem poles were made by many Northwest Coast groups. Here, Haida totem poles stare out at the sea in 1885.

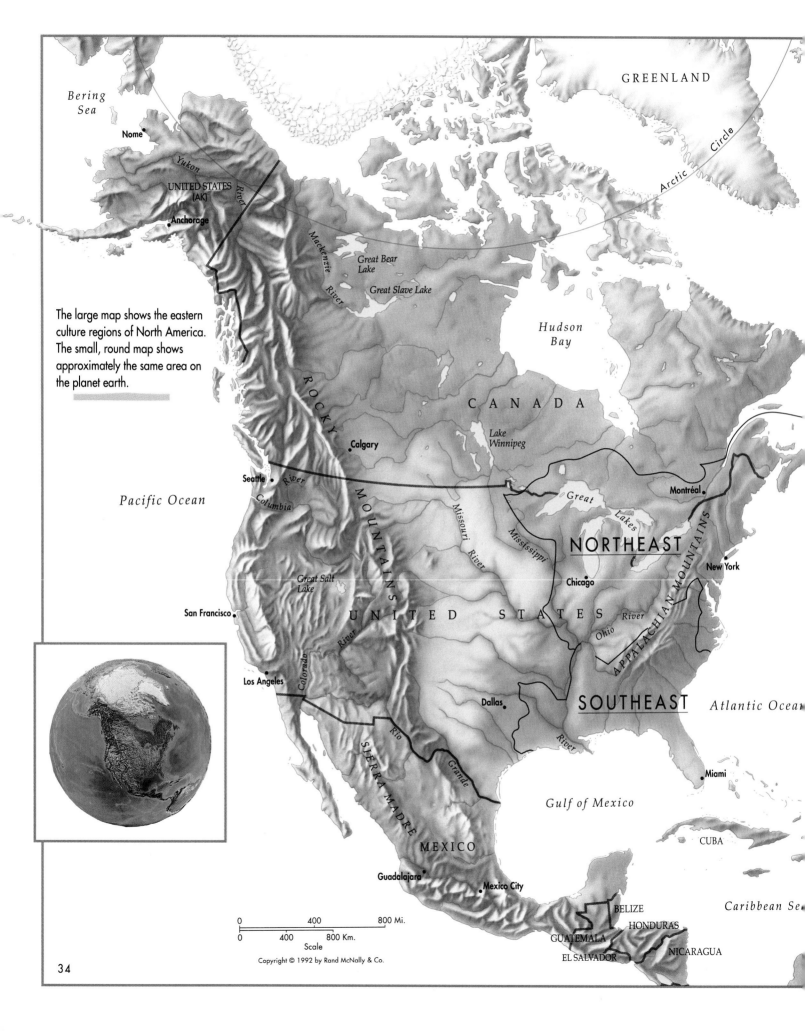

Bering
Sea

GREENLAND

Nome

Arctic Circle

Yukon

UNITED STATES
(AK)

River

Anchorage

Mackenzie

River

Great Bear
Lake

Great Slave Lake

Hudson
Bay

The large map shows the eastern
culture regions of North America.
The small, round map shows
approximately the same area on
the planet earth.

C A N A D A

Calgary

Lake
Winnipeg

ROCKY

Seattle

River

Montréal

Columbia

Great

Pacific Ocean

MOUNTAINS

Missouri

Lakes

NORTHEAST

Mississippi

APPALACHIAN MOUNTAINS

New York

Chicago

Great Salt
Lake

U N I T E D   S T A T E S

Ohio   River

San Francisco

River

SOUTHEAST

Atlantic Ocean

Colorado

Los Angeles

Dallas

Rio

Miami

SIERRA MADRE

Grande

River

Gulf of Mexico

CUBA

MEXICO

Guadalajara

Mexico City

Caribbean Se

BELIZE

0   400   800 Mi.

HONDURAS

0   400   800 Km.

GUATEMALA

NICARAGUA

Scale

EL SALVADOR

34

TRIBES OF THE EAST

A Powhatan family works in front of a multifamily dwelling. The house was created with arched saplings covered with bark and woven mats, which could be removed. Tall, ripening corn grows in a nearby plot.

POWHATAN AND MASSACHUSET

The American Indians of the northeastern woodlands lived in small, permanent settlements situated along rivers, seacoasts, and marshes. Although crops such as corn, beans, and squash were important, the cold weather and short growing season of the Northeast and the Great Lakes areas limited farming activities. But the woodland areas provided a rich diet.

These Native Americans collected sap from maple trees in early spring, then boiled off the water to make maple syrup. Plant leaves were gathered in the spring, and berries, nuts, and roots later in the year. They fished the waterways in every season but winter; hunting was best in the fall. Game included rabbit, squirrel, beaver, turkey, duck, and goose, but deer was most important. They preserved some of this meat for storage by smoking it. American Indians along the Atlantic coast gathered shellfish, and those in the Great Lakes region took advantage of abundant wild rice.

Native Americans of the Northeast lived in two basic types of house: the *longhouse*, used by the Iroquois, and the *wigwam*, used by the Algonquian. Longhouses were made with log frames and were sometimes over a hundred feet long. Wigwams were created

A Massachuset woman poses in her traditional dress in 1923.

OJIBWA

MN

Lake Superior

MI

WI

Lake Michigan

Mississippi

IA

IL

Chicago

MO

River

AR

MS

AZ

by driving a circle of wooden poles into the ground, then tying the poles together with bark strips from birch or elm trees. The resulting dome-shaped framework was covered with bark, reeds, or mats of woven plants.

The forest provided Northeast Indians with raw material for the dugouts and bark-covered canoes used to travel the region's many waterways. Wood was also used to make the frames of snowshoes, which helped hunters outrun their larger prey in winter.

The Powhatan were an Algonquian-speaking group who lived in what is now Virginia. They were the first Native Americans to live side-by-side with English settlers, who in 1607 founded their first colony at Jamestown. Shortly before these Europeans arrived, a chief named Powhatan established a powerful confederacy composed of thirty separate Indian bands and two hundred villages. Member tribes helped the Powhatan in times of war and paid taxes—such as food, furs, and pearls—to their chief. Relations between the settlers and the Powhatan began peacefully, but hostilities developed as the settlers took more and more land. The daughter of Chief Powhatan, known best by the nickname Pocahontas, supposedly saved the life of Captain John Smith, the Jamestown leader, when he was captured. This began a decade of peace between the Powhatan and the colonists.

In what is now New England, the Algonquian-speaking Massachuset Indians formed a less rigid confederacy of several related tribal groups. They lived along the valleys of rivers in the area, including the site of Boston and its suburbs in present-day Massachusetts. They relied heavily on cod and shellfish but also cultivated corn and squash in fields usually located near rivers. Today, little is known about Massachuset culture because it disappeared before historians could record it. European diseases, especially smallpox, devastated these and other Native Americans. Wars with neighboring tribes also reduced their number.

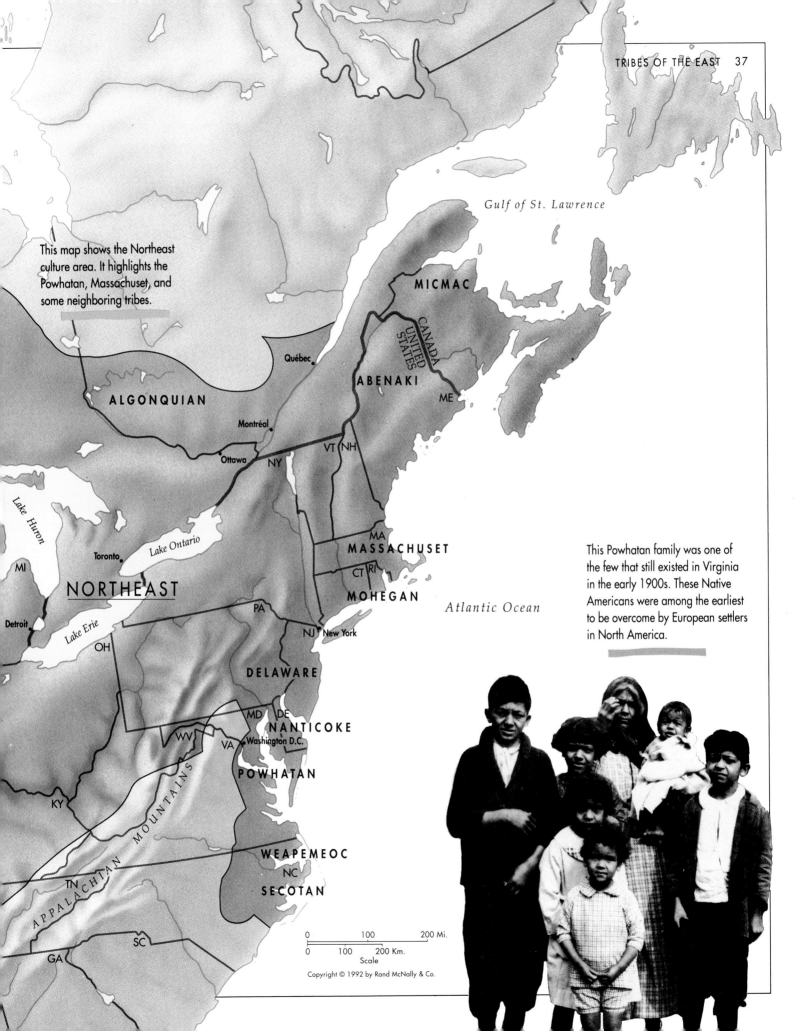

Gulf of St. Lawrence

This map shows the Northeast culture area. It highlights the Powhatan, Massachuset, and some neighboring tribes.

MICMAC

CANADA
UNITED STATES

ABENAKI

Québec

ALGONQUIAN

ME

Montréal

VT NH

Ottawa

NY

Lake Huron

Toronto

Lake Ontario

MA

MASSACHUSET

MI

CT RI

NORTHEAST

MOHEGAN

Atlantic Ocean

Detroit

Lake Erie

OH

PA

NJ New York

DELAWARE

This Powhatan family was one of the few that still existed in Virginia in the early 1900s. These Native Americans were among the earliest to be overcome by European settlers in North America.

MD DE
NANTICOKE

WV

VA Washington D.C.

POWHATAN

KY

APPALACHIAN MOUNTAINS

TN

WEAPEMEOC

NC

SECOTAN

SC

GA

| 0 | 100 | 200 Mi. |
| 0 | 100 | 200 Km. |

Scale

Hudson Bay

IROQUOIS, OJIBWA, AND MENOMINEE

Surrounded by Algonquian-speaking tribes, the Native Americans of what is now approximately upper New York State formed an island of Iroquois-speaking peoples. Together these tribes—the Seneca, Cayuga, Oneida, Onondaga, Mohawk, and Tuscarora—are known as the Iroquois.

Each Iroquois village typically held several hundred people. The typical Iroquois dwelling, the *longhouse*, was a rectangular structure with straight sides and an arched or slanted roof, often covered with elm bark. These dwellings were about twenty feet (six meters) wide, but could be anywhere from fifty to two hundred feet (fifteen to sixty meters) long, depending on the number of families living in them. Fires were placed in the center so that two families, one on either side of the longhouse, could share each one. A typical longhouse held ten families.

The Iroquois depended on agriculture more than any other group in the region, but they also gathered wild plants and hunted to supplement the food they grew. Women held much power in Iroquois society. They chose leaders, owned crops, and passed on the family name. Men built houses, fought wars, hunted, and fished.

Sometime before 1600, the Iroquois-speaking groups united peacefully. The resulting confederation, called the

OJIBWA

MN

Lake Superior

MI

MENOMINEE

WI

POTAWATOMI

Lake Michigan

Lake Huron

MI

Toro

NEUTR

NORTHEAST

Detroit

Lake Erie

OH

ERIE

MIAMI

IL

IN

Chicago

Mississippi

IA

ILLINOIS

MO

SHAWNEE

KY

River

TN

APPALACHIA

AR

MS

AL

GA

SD

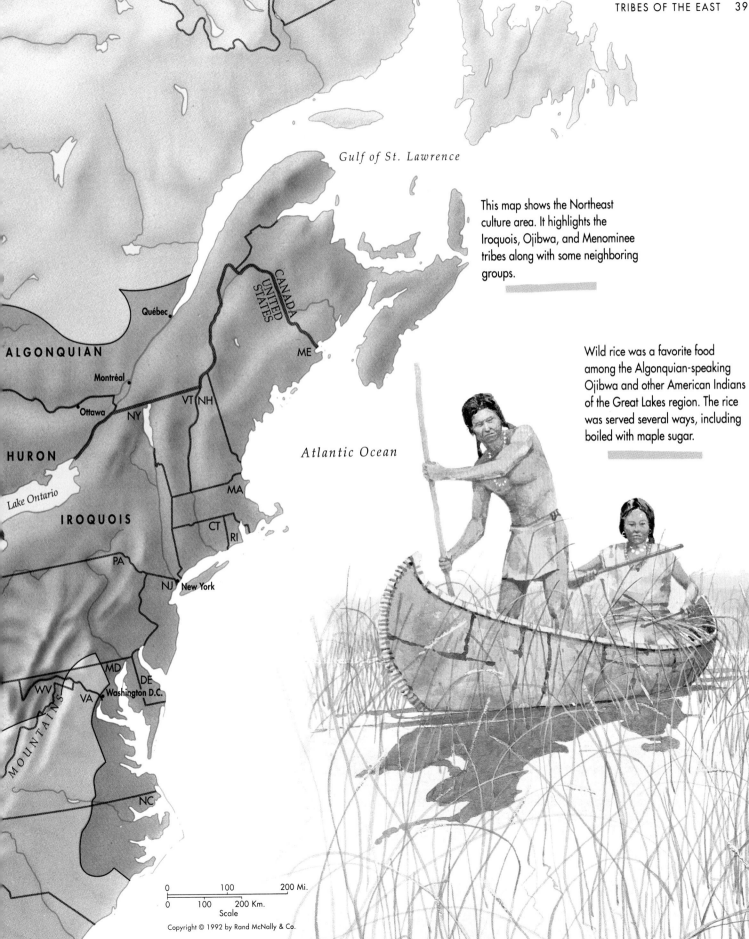

Gulf of St. Lawrence

ALGONQUIAN

Québec

Montréal

Ottawa

NY

VT NH

ME

HURON

Lake Ontario

Atlantic Ocean

CANADA
UNITED
STATES

IROQUOIS

MA

CT
RI

PA

NJ New York

MD

WV

DE

VA Washington D.C.

M O U N T A I N S

NC

This map shows the Northeast culture area. It highlights the Iroquois, Ojibwa, and Menominee tribes along with some neighboring groups.

Wild rice was a favorite food among the Algonquian-speaking Ojibwa and other American Indians of the Great Lakes region. The rice was served several ways, including boiled with maple sugar.

0   100   200 Mi.
0   100   200 Km.
Scale

Copyright © 1992 by Rand McNally & Co.

With the top of a Menominee lodge folded back, there is a better view of the Medicine Dance taking place inside. The term "medicine" here means supernatural power, as well as the ability to cure the sick.

Iroquois League, was the best organized and most powerful Indian group in the Northeast. Peace among the Iroquois did not, however, mean peace with neighbors. Throughout the 1600s, the Iroquois League fought a series of wars with other Native American groups.

The Ojibwa, better known as the Chippewa in the United States, were a powerful Algonquian-speaking group that dominated the northern Great Lakes region. Each tribe was divided into migrating bands. In the fall, these bands separated into families that moved to the hunting grounds, gathering together again in the summer at the fishing grounds. These hunters grew small amounts of corn, pumpkin, and squash, but a more important food was the wild rice they gathered along the shores of waterways.

Some Ojibwa groups lived a different life-style. Those north of the Great Lakes lived as Subarctic tribes and are considered part of the Subarctic culture area. To the west, where Ojibwa lands bordered on the northern plains, some groups adopted the bison-hunting life-style of the Plains Indians.

The Menominee Indians of northern Wisconsin lived a more settled life-style than the Ojibwa, occupying permanent villages of wigwams. A major food source for many Great Lakes Indians was especially abundant in the marshes along the waterways of Menominee territory—so long hunting trips were not as important. The plant is really a tall grass with an edible, rice-like seed. Like some Ojibwa, the Menominee gathered this "wild rice" in the early fall. Navigating the rice beds in canoes, they would bend the plant stalks over and strike them with *ricing sticks*, tapping the ripened grain into the boat's bottom.

This Mohawk woman is weaving in front of a birchbark canoe. The Mohawks were part of the powerful Iroquois League.

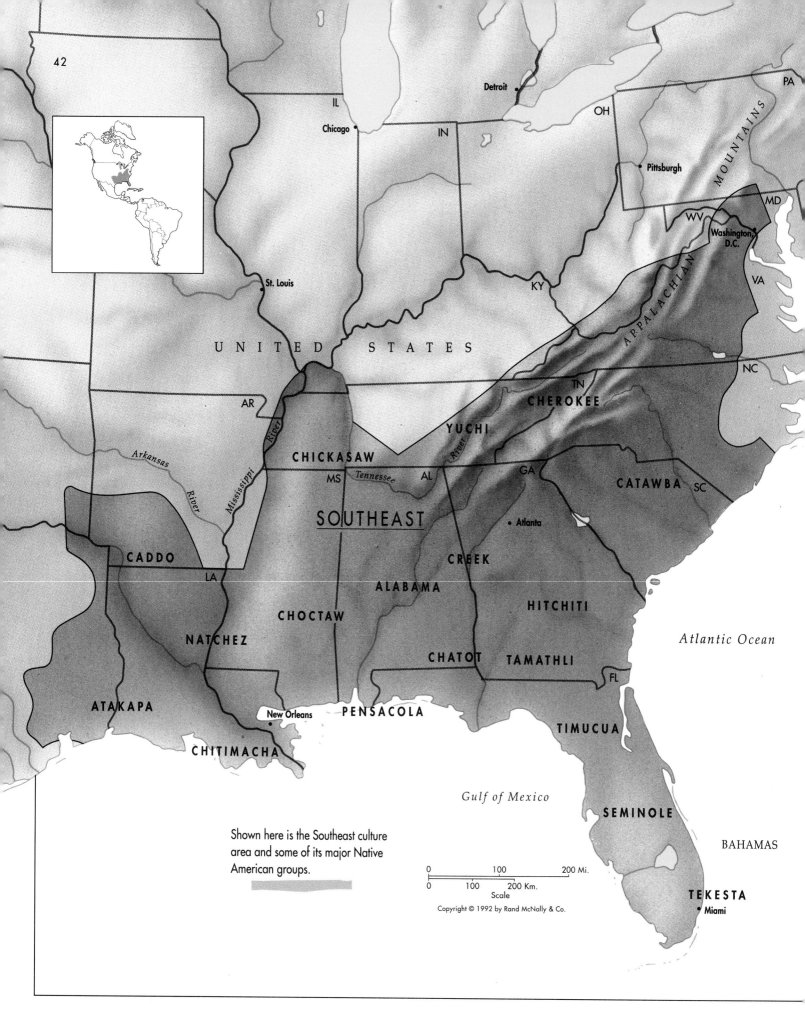

PA

Detroit

OH

Chicago

IN

Pittsburgh

MD

WV

Washington
D.C.

VA

St. Louis

KY

NC

U N I T E D   S T A T E S

TN

CHEROKEE

AR

YUCHI

APPALACHIAN

Arkansas

MOUNTAINS

CHICKASAW

MS

Tennessee

AL

GA

CATAWBA

SC

Tennessee River

Mississippi River

River

SOUTHEAST

Atlanta

CADDO

CREEK

LA

ALABAMA

HITCHITI

CHOCTAW

Atlantic Ocean

NATCHEZ

CHATOT

TAMATHLI

FL

ATAKAPA

New Orleans

PENSACOLA

TIMUCUA

CHITIMACHA

SEMINOLE

Gulf of Mexico

BAHAMAS

Shown here is the Southeast culture
area and some of its major Native
American groups.

TEKESTA

Miami

0   100   200 Mi.

0   100   200 Km.
Scale

Copyright © 1992 by Rand McNally & Co.

New York

delphia

CHEROKEE, CREEK, AND SEMINOLE

The people of the Southeast culture area were descended from the ancient Mound Builders. They developed what is thought to be the most advanced culture north of Mexico. The plentiful wildlife and edible plants of the region, along with a mild climate favorable for agriculture, supported the large-scale settlements of southeastern tribes.

After the other Native Americans drove them out of the Great Lakes area, the Iroquois-speaking Cherokee settled in the Southeast along the Appalachian Mountains. With over two hundred villages—and a population of some twenty-two thousand in the mid-1600s—they were the largest and most powerful group in the region. Each village contained between thirty and sixty log houses. Like other Southeast groups, Cherokee villages formed a confederacy of "red towns," in which war ceremonies were held, and "white towns" for peace rituals.

The Cherokee used bows and arrows to hunt large game, such as bear and deer. They used blow guns to kill squirrels, rabbits, and turkeys. Corn, beans, squash, and sunflowers grew well in the dark, rich soil. The dense forests held many edible plants.

The Creek occupied the flatlands of present-day Georgia and Alabama. The name *Creek* is an English word for several different groups. The Muskogee, or Upper Creek, occupied the northern lands. The Hitchiti and Alabama, in the southern region, came to be called the Lower Creek. Creek women did most of the farming, growing beans, corn, and squash, while the men hunted.

A small group of Seminoles remained in the Florida Everglades after the other American Indians were removed from the Southeast. This Seminole man spears a fish from his dugout canoe in the Everglades in about 1940. He is wearing traditional Seminole garb.

A Creek man posed for this portrait about one hundred years ago.

There were about fifty Creek villages, each with a central plaza surrounded by houses formed by wooden walls and plaster. Within the plaza of many Creek towns sat a temple-topped earthen pyramid that looked like the stone temple-pyramids of many Mexican groups. Some people believe that the American Indians of the Southeast and those of Mexico had contact with one another.

The plaza was a gathering place for festivals. The most important among southeastern Native Americans was the midsummer Green Corn Festival. As a part of this festival, every crime except murder was forgiven. To prepare for this ceremony, men repaired and women cleaned buildings—sometimes even burning some of their possessions. The most important villagers fasted, then gathered for a great feast.

The name *Seminole* comes from a Creek word meaning "runaway." In the 1750s migrants from Lower Creek towns moved southward. They joined American Indians who had inhabited the Florida Everglades for generations. By the 1800s, all these Native Americans became known as Seminoles. They built their villages along the rivers that ran through swamplands. They cultivated some plants, but mostly they hunted and fished for a living. For shelter, they built simple open dwellings from poles and plants.

In the 1830s, the Cherokee, Creek, Seminole, Choctaw, and Chickasaw—later known as the Five Civilized Tribes—were forced from their homelands. They were brutally mistreated by white people and moved to what was then called Indian Territory (now Oklahoma). The trip was so terrible, the Cherokee referred to the path they took to Oklahoma as the Trail of Tears. Small groups managed to remain in their homelands, particularly some Cherokee and Seminole.

These Cherokee women were part of the small group that managed to remain in the mountains of North Carolina while the others were removed to Oklahoma in 1838. The Great Smoky Mountains are still home to some Cherokee.

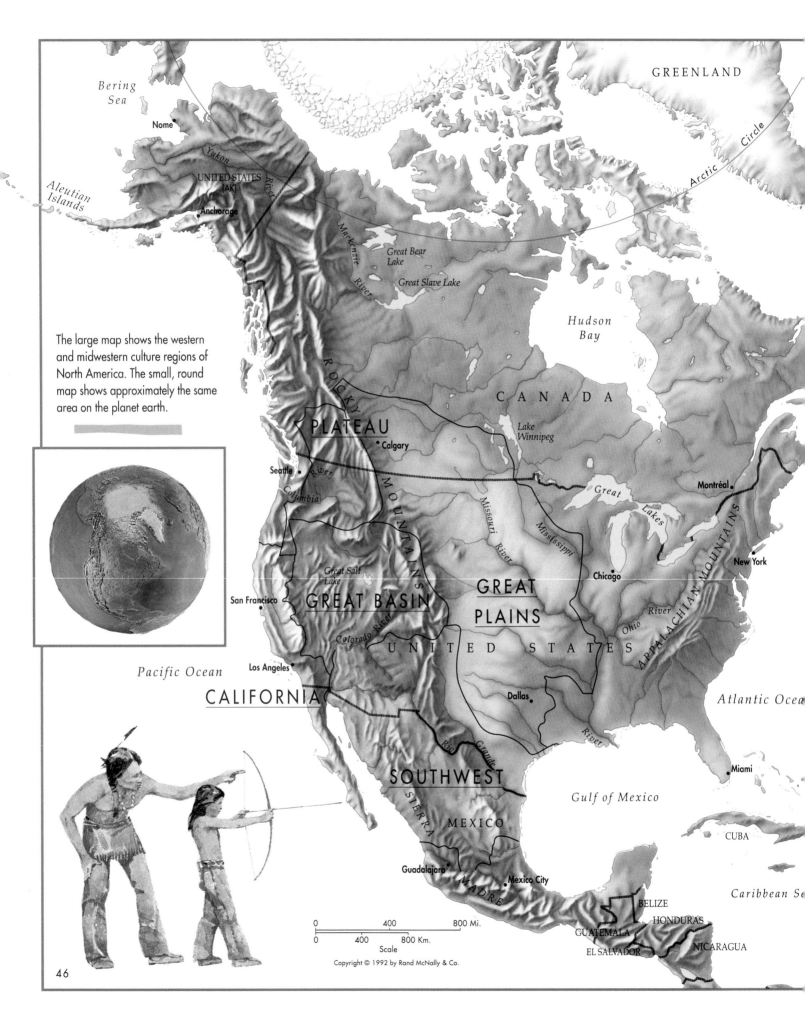

The large map shows the western and midwestern culture regions of North America. The small, round map shows approximately the same area on the planet earth.

GREENLAND

Bering Sea

Nome

Aleutian Islands

Yukon River

UNITED STATES (AK)

Anchorage

Arctic Circle

Mackenzie River

Great Bear Lake

Great Slave Lake

Hudson Bay

ROCKY MOUNTAINS

PLATEAU

Calgary

Seattle

Columbia River

C A N A D A

Lake Winnipeg

Montréal

Great Lakes

San Francisco

GREAT BASIN

Great Salt Lake

Missouri River

Mississippi

GREAT PLAINS

Chicago

Ohio River

APPALACHIAN MOUNTAINS

New York

Colorado River

U N I T E D   S T A T E S

Los Angeles

Pacific Ocean

CALIFORNIA

Dallas

Atlantic Ocean

SOUTHWEST

Rio Grande

River

Miami

SIERRA

Gulf of Mexico

MEXICO

CUBA

Guadalajara

MADRE

Mexico City

Caribbean Sea

BELIZE

HONDURAS

GUATEMALA

EL SALVADOR

NICARAGUA

0   400   800 Mi.

0   400   800 Km.

Scale

GREAT PLAINS AND WESTERN TRIBES

THE PEOPLE OF THE PLAINS

Stretching from the Rocky Mountains to the Mississippi River, from southern Canada to the Gulf of Mexico, the rolling grasslands of the Great Plains held some sixty million bison, or buffalo, that roamed freely in enormous herds. Dozens of American Indian groups depended on this incredible resource: the Arapaho, Blackfeet, Cheyenne, Crow, Iowa, Pawnee, Sioux, Plains Cree, and many more. These were the peoples of the Plains.

Plains Indians may be the most familiar to us today. But the culture we know did not emerge until long after the arrival of Europeans, specifically the Spanish who explored far into the Americas in the 1500s. The horses they brought and then left behind reshaped the bison-hunting life-style that characterized the Native Americans of this region.

When the Spanish explorer Francisco de Coronado encountered some of the southern Plains tribes in 1541, he found nomadic bison hunters—people who roamed from place to place with the herds. Dogs were the only pack animals. So while the arrival of the horse did not actually create the

Many Sioux groups existed on the Great Plains. The three main groups were the Lakota, Nakota, and Dakota. Like other Plains hunters, the Sioux relied heavily on the bison.

47

nomadic Plains life-style, it did become much easier. Horses gave these Native Americans the ability to search a wide area for bison herds. Since horses could outrun bison, the animals could be killed more efficiently. More time could be spent on other activities, like making clothing, carrying out rituals, and raiding other American Indian groups.

Foraging nomads had lived along the rivers of the Great Plains for thousands of years, but they apparently left the area around AD 1200. After that, the farming peoples who occupied the fertile prairies along the Missouri River—the Pawnee, Arikara, Wichita, Mandan, and Hidatsa—were probably the first to settle in the Plains.

The Mandan, who lived in what is now North Dakota, were typical of these prairie farmers. They lived in villages of up to one hundred *earth lodges* enclosed by strong walls of upright logs. An earth lodge began as a shallow circular pit. Posts were placed around the outside to help form the walls, and others were used as roof supports. The Indians then banked a thick layer of earth to form the walls and covered willow mats with earth to complete the roof. Usually between twenty and forty people shared each house.

The Mandan cultivated maize, squash, and sunflowers; fished; and hunted deer, elk, bear, and other game. But the bison hunt was an important event for every village. When scouts warned of an

Fellow members of a Hidatsa group look on as Dog Society warriors perform a ceremony. Members of the society were "contraries" and did everything "backwards." If a Dog Society member said "yes," for example, he really meant "no."

PLAINS CREE

BLACKFEET

Calgary

Regina

PLAINS OJIBWA

Winnipeg

WA

CANADA
UNITED STATES

GROS VENTRE

ASSINIBOIN

ND

MN

Lake Superior

HIDATSA

MANDAN

WI

OR

CROW

MT

SD

Minneapolis

Lake Michigan

WY

CHEYENNE

SIOUX

ID

GREAT PLAINS

IA

CA

NV

NE

IL

Chicago

IN

OMAHA

PAWNEE

IOWA

Missouri

ROCKY MOUNTAINS

UT

CO

Denver

MO

MISSOURI

River

St. Louis

ARAPAHO

KS

KANSA

Shown here is the Great Plains
culture area and some of its major
American Indian groups.

NM

KIOWA

OK

OSAGE

AR

TN

TX

Arkansas

River

QUAPAW

MS

WICHITA

Dallas

LA

Mississippi River

COMANCHE

Houston

New Orleans

UNITED STATES
MEXICO

Pacific Ocean

Gulf of Mexico

0   200   400 Mi.

0   200   400 Km.

Scale

Copyright © 1992 by Rand McNally & Co.

approaching herd, Mandan villagers set up traps that allowed them to stampede the bison to the edge of a cliff or into an enclosure. These Native Americans did not waste any part of their bison catch. The meat of the bison fed the tribe. Its hide was used to cover the portable, cone-shaped dwellings called *tepee*s and for shields, moccasins, and bull-boats. The animal's bones and horns became tools and cups. After they acquired the horse, the prairie farmers spent part of the year on the plains hunting bison and part in their villages.

Only a few nonfarming American Indian groups, such as the Blackfeet, lived in the drier western regions before about 1500. Later many other tribes migrated into the Plains—the Arapaho, Comanche, Cheyenne, Plains Cree, Plains Ojibwa, Kiowa, Sacree, Crow, Sioux, and others—and adopted the Plains life-style.

Winter on the Great Plains did not stop these Mandan villagers from a game of *chunkey*, played with a disk and spears.

The Comanche broke away from the Wind River Shoshone of Wyoming to settle in western Texas. One of the first American Indian groups to acquire horses, the Comanche kept huge herds and were expert horse trainers. Horses were valuable, and horse stealing between Native American groups became a major reason for war. Usually warfare involved small raiding parties to steal horses, avenge a death, protect hunting grounds, or to acquire glory. Bravery in battle was often established by simply touching an enemy's body without hurting him. This could be done with the hand or with a weapon, but usually was accomplished with a *coup stick*.

Trading between American Indian groups was common. Nomads might exchange goods for the grain produced by the farming peoples, for instance. The Cheyenne played an important role in the horse trade between southern tribes like the Comanche and the Indians of the northern Plains. Items introduced in the Northeast by the French and British—such as cloth, kettles, and guns—were so valued by some groups in the southern Plains that they would trade horses for them.

With the advance of white settlers in the Great Plains in the 1800s, many Plains Indians participated in the Ghost Dance. The dance was intended to restore the traditional Native American way of life. Here a group of Arapaho perform the Ghost Dance in 1893.

This Blackfeet woman sits for a portrait in 1900. She carries her children on a *travois* behind her. In the background are some of the tepees of her community.

These Western Shoshone forage the Great Basin for roots and seeds. The desert environment provided a hard life for these Native Americans.

SHOSHONE, UTE, AND PAIUTE

A vast, bowl-shaped desert region sits in the western part of the United States, in the region that contains the Great Salt Lake in Utah. Flanked by the Rocky Mountains and the Sierra Nevada, this region is known as the Great Basin. Its deepest depression, Death Valley in California's Mojave Desert, marks the lowest point in the Americas. Temperatures there can be scorching—up to 134° F (57° C), the highest temperature ever recorded in the Western Hemisphere.

The Great Basin region provided unique challenges to the American Indians who settled there. Only low grasses, sagebrush, juniper trees, and other plants adapted to the dry climate could grow. Antelope, jackrabbits, mice, rats, gophers, snakes, lizards, birds, and even grasshoppers provided food for the Native Americans of the Great Basin. They traveled in small bands, roving the desert in search of the scarce food it could supply. They lived in temporary cone-shaped dwellings fashioned from brush-covered poles.

The Shoshone, Ute, and Paiute shared this foraging life-style. The Shoshone were typical foragers. Family groups would scatter in search of food during the summer, gathering together in the fall and winter for festivals and hunts. Local groups rarely grew larger than fifty people. There were no chiefs, but skilled individuals led festivals, hunting parties, and wars.

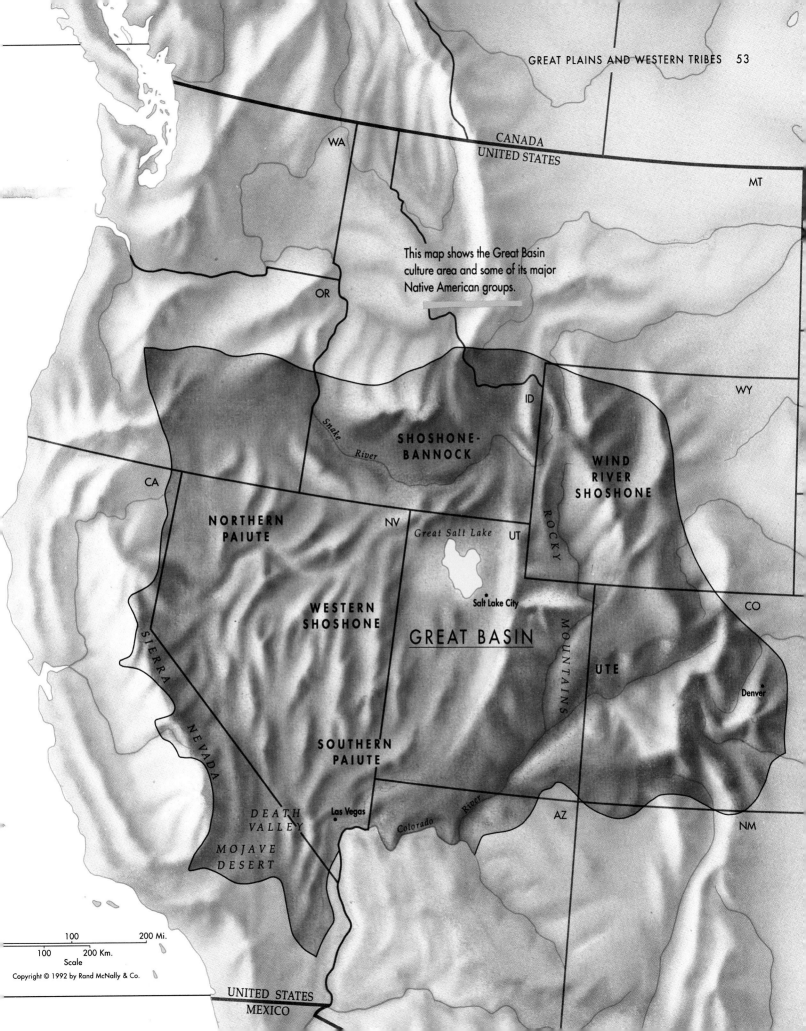

WA

CANADA
UNITED STATES

MT

OR

This map shows the Great Basin
culture area and some of its major
Native American groups.

Snake

WY

River

SHOSHONE-
BANNOCK

ID

WIND
RIVER
SHOSHONE

CA

NORTHERN
PAIUTE

NV

Great Salt Lake

UT

R
O
C
K
Y

Salt Lake City

CO

WESTERN
SHOSHONE

GREAT BASIN

M
O
U
N
T
A
I
N
S

UTE

Denver

S
I
E
R
R
A

SOUTHERN
PAIUTE

N
E
V
A
D
A

*D E A T H
V A L L E Y*

Las Vegas

Colorado

River

AZ

NM

*M O J A V E
D E S E R T*

100   200 Mi.

100   200 Km.
Scale

UNITED STATES
MEXICO

American Indian games were basically of two types: games of chance and games of skill. Here a group of Paiute men in Utah play a game in the 1870s.

The Northern Shoshone, who lived in present-day Wyoming and Idaho, hunted game in the forests that flanked the Rockies. They also fished the rivers for salmon like the American Indians of the Plateau region farther north. Like the Wind River Shoshone, they acquired horses in the late 1600s and adopted a new life-style. They began to live more like the Plains Indians, hunting bison and antelope and living in tepees.

Another Great Basin group, the Ute, lived in the region from eastern Colorado into northern New Mexico, northeastern Arizona, and Utah. In fact, the state of Utah takes its name from this tribe. The Ute harvested wild seeds and roots, organized rabbit and antelope hunts, and fished the rivers streaming west from the Rockies. The Ute lived in shelters made from a pole framework covered with brush. As with the neighboring Shoshone, the arrival of horses changed their life-style, but they retained their traditional ways until the late 1800s. They began raiding the Pueblo Indians and Europeans in New Mexico for livestock, but the Ute rarely hunted bison.

The Northern Paiute lived in parts of Oregon, Idaho, Nevada, Utah, and California and were distinctly different from the related Ute and Southern Paiute. The Northern Paiute hunted small animals and birds, foraged for plants such as pine nuts or cattails, and made baskets for

Shown here is a Northern Shoshone village in 1870. These American Indians adopted elements of the Plains Indian life-style when they acquired horses in the 1600s.

seed collecting and storage. The temporary dwellings they built from brush-covered willow poles were very similar to Apache *wickiups*. An offshoot of the Northern Paiute, the Bannock, hunted bison with the Shoshone in what is now southern Idaho.

The Southern Paiute, who lived in parts of Utah, Arizona, Nevada, and California, shared not only the foraging life-style of the Ute but their language as well. They supplemented their diet with the corn and squash they grew in small gardens.

This Ute household was photographed in Utah in the 1870s. Because they were wanderers, Ute dwellings were temporary. The climate was hot, so little shelter was needed. The Great Basin groups were expert basket weavers.

KLAMATH

Between the Cascade Range in the west and the Rocky Mountains in the east lies the Columbia Plateau. This region, in which the Plateau culture existed, occupies parts of what is now the northwestern United States and southwestern Canada.

Grass and sagebrush cover the flatlands of the dry central part of the plateau, while dense forests of spruce, fir, pine, and cedar trees flank the mountains. From the grasslands the Plateau Indians ate wild onions, wild carrots, and the roots of the camas plant (a lily). At the edge of the forest they stalked elk, rabbit, or bear. But food was most plentiful near the waterways. The yearly runs of the salmon, which swim upriver to lay their eggs, made for an easy catch.

The Klamath occupied the shores of marshes and lakes in what is now south-central Oregon. They lived in pit houses, log frames covered with saplings, reeds, and mud and placed over holes in the ground. These houses were cool in the summer and warm in the winter. The Klamath traveled the lakes and rivers of their homeland in dugout canoes.

Excellent with bow and arrow, the Klamaths frequently raided tribes in northern California, taking captives that they either kept as slaves or sold to other Indian groups. After European contact and the introduction of the horse in the 1500s, many tribes of the eastern Plateau used horses to hunt bison and adopted a life-style similar to that of the Plains Indians.

The fate of the Klamath was the same as that of many American Indians. In the 1860s, they signed a treaty creating a reservation of their homeland.

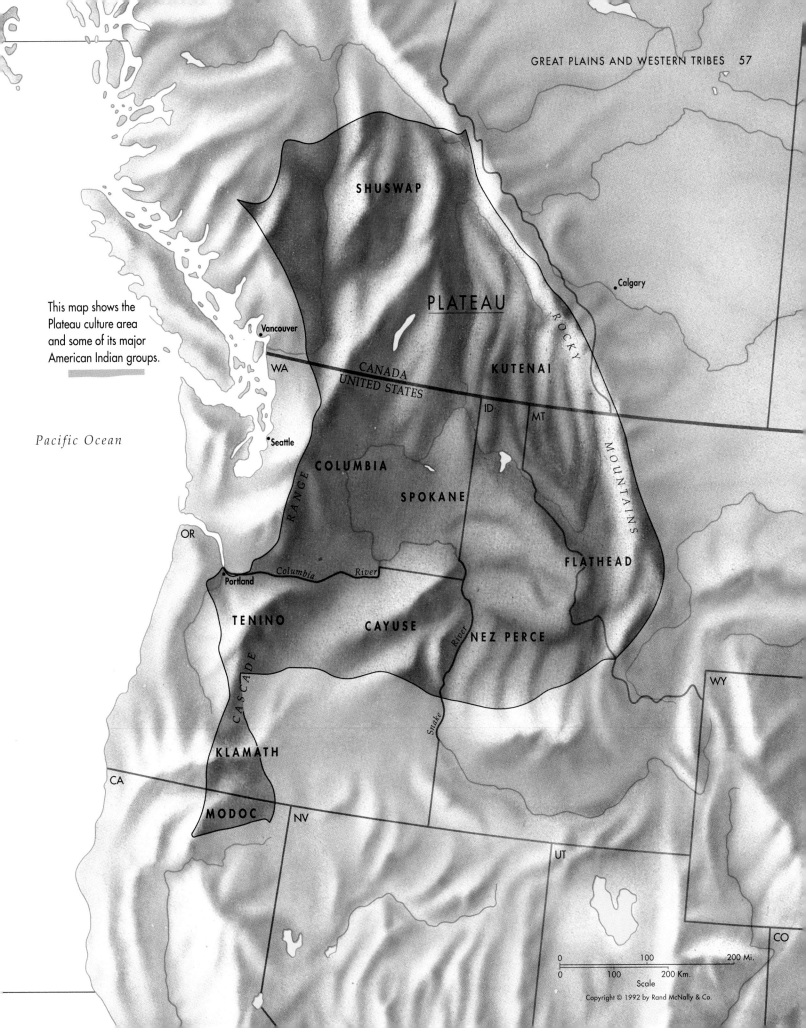

This map shows the Plateau culture area and some of its major American Indian groups.

Pacific Ocean

SHUSWAP

PLATEAU

Calgary

KUTENAI

Vancouver

CANADA
UNITED STATES

WA

Seattle

COLUMBIA

SPOKANE

ROCKY

ID   MT

MOUNTAINS

RANGE

OR

FLATHEAD

Columbia   River

Portland

TENINO

CAYUSE

NEZ PERCE

River

CASCADE

Snake

River

WY

KLAMATH

CA

MODOC   NV

UT

CO

0   100   200 Mi.
0   100   200 Km.
Scale

Copyright © 1992 by Rand McNally & Co.

Made from wooden planks, the boats of California's Chumash Indians were unique in North America. From these boats, the Chumash were able to catch a great variety of ocean fish, shellfish, and mammals such as seals.

CHUMASH

The mild weather and rich, varied landscape of what is now California helped create a thriving American Indian population. There were many different native Californians—in fact, over two hundred dialects were spoken in the region.

One trait these Native Americans shared was a foraging life-style. The land provided such plenty, they had no need for farming. They hunted deer, rabbit, and duck, and gathered berries, nuts, seeds, and roots. Their diet even included insects such as caterpillars and grasshoppers.

The acorn was one of the most important foods in the region. The Indians sun-dried the kernels, pounded them into a powder, and then washed the powder to remove the bitter taste. The result was a flour they could use in a soup or bake into bread. Coastal Indians added fish and other seafood to their diet.

One of these coastal groups was the Chumash, who lived in the region between present-day San Luis Obispo and Los Angeles. Throughout California, Indians built rafts or made dugout canoes to transport supplies along waterways. But the Chumash were the only people in North America to build their boats from wooden

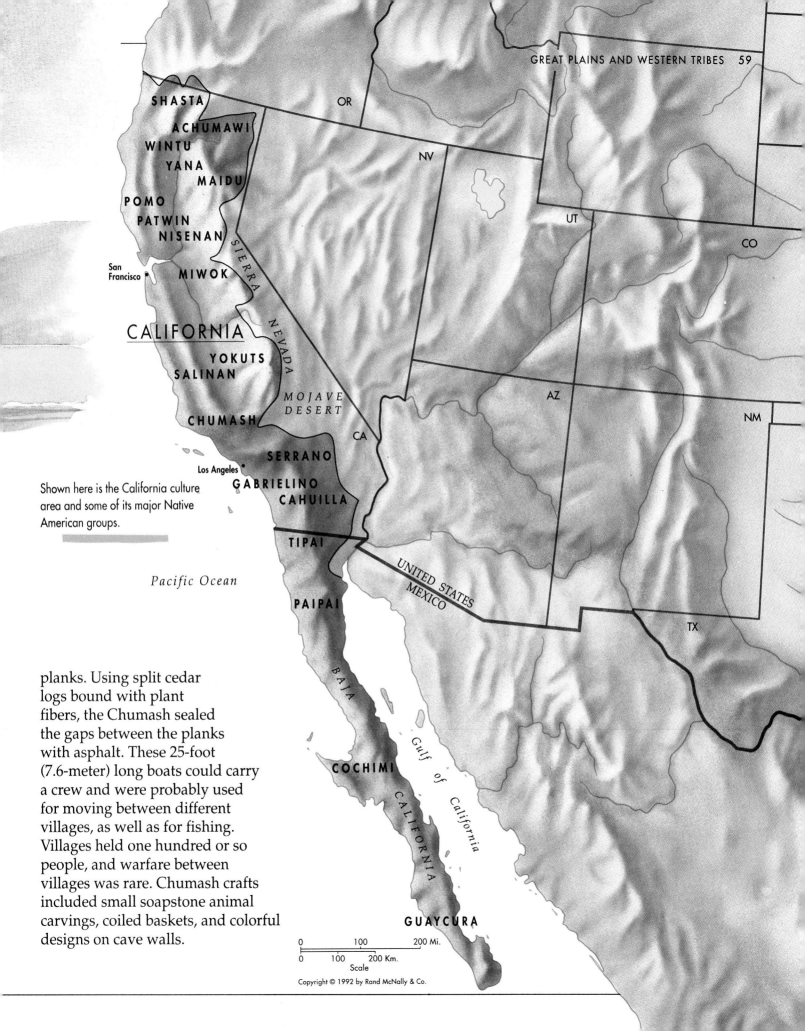

OR

NV

UT

CO

AZ

NM

TX

SHASTA

ACHUMAWI

WINTU

YANA

MAIDU

POMO

PATWIN

NISENAN

San
Francisco

MIWOK

SIERRA

NEVADA

CALIFORNIA

YOKUTS

SALINAN

*MOJAVE
DESERT*

CHUMASH

CA

SERRANO

Los Angeles

GABRIELINO

CAHUILLA

Shown here is the California culture
area and some of its major Native
American groups.

TIPAI

Pacific Ocean

UNITED STATES

MEXICO

PAIPAI

BAJA

planks. Using split cedar
logs bound with plant
fibers, the Chumash sealed
the gaps between the planks
with asphalt. These 25-foot
(7.6-meter) long boats could carry
a crew and were probably used
for moving between different
villages, as well as for fishing.
Villages held one hundred or so
people, and warfare between
villages was rare. Chumash crafts
included small soapstone animal
carvings, coiled baskets, and colorful
designs on cave walls.

COCHIMI

*Gulf
of
California*

CALIFORNIA

GUAYCURA

0	100	200 Mi.
0	100	200 Km.

Scale

Here a Navajo man tends his sheep in present-day Monument Valley, Arizona. Today, the Navajo are the largest North American Indian group in terms of population and in area of reservation lands.

Expert silversmiths and weavers, Navajos here practice their artistry. They learned how to weave with wool after the Spanish introduced sheep to the Southwest. Earlier in this century, they learned how to work silver. Behind is a hogan, a typical Navajo dwelling.

APACHE, NAVAJO, AND HOPI

The rugged lands of the Southwest culture area held tribes with very different life-styles. Some, like the Apache and Navajo, were nomadic hunter-gatherers, while others, like the Hopi and Zuni, were desert farmers.

The Apache and Navajo arrived in the Southwest much later than other Indians, perhaps as recently as one thousand years ago. Their Athapascan languages are similar to that spoken by Native Americans in northwestern Canada. Scholars believe the Apache and Navajo settled in the Southwest after a long migration from the north.

The word *Apache* comes from a Zuni word meaning "enemy." Both the Apache and Navajo led frequent raids on the farming villages of the Hopi and Zuni when they could not find enough food in their own lands. Like many other American Indian groups, the Apache named themselves using a word in their own language that translated into English as "the people."

The most common Apache dwelling was the *wickiup*, a domed or cone-shaped frame covered with grass or brush. In general, the Apache gathered whatever game and edible plants they could find, but different Apache bands had different life-styles.

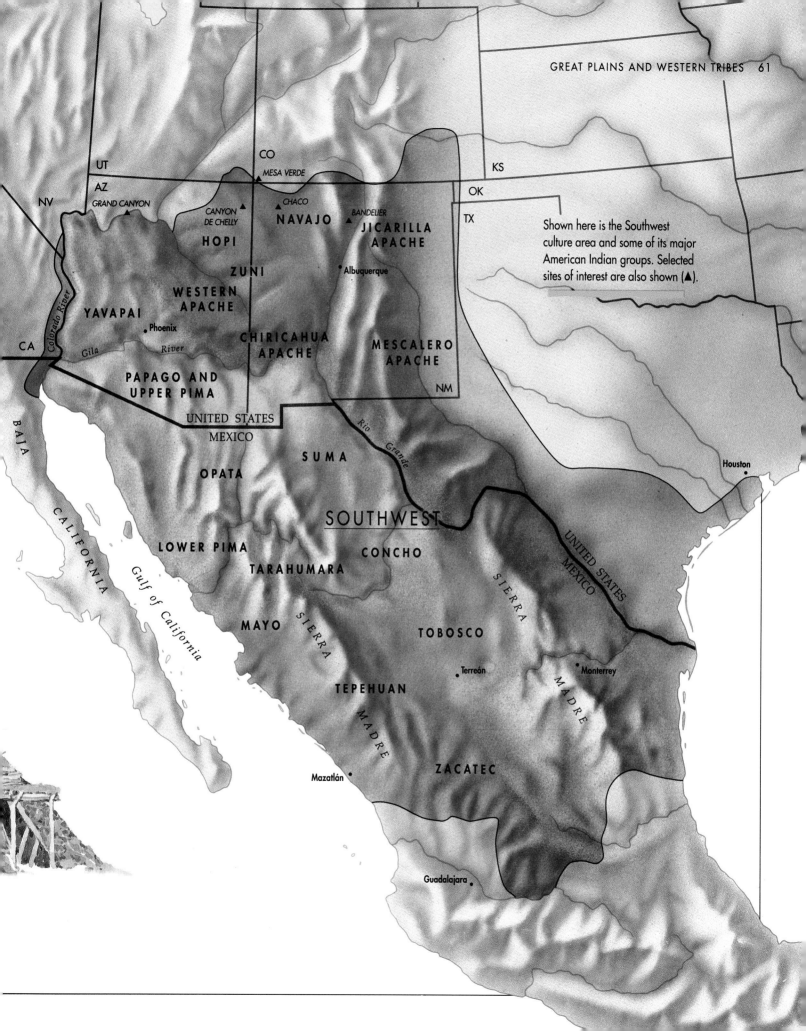

UT

NV

AZ

CA

CO

MESA VERDE ▲

GRAND CANYON ▲

CANYON DE CHELLY ▲

CHACO ▲

BANDELIER ▲

KS

OK

TX

NM

Shown here is the Southwest culture area and some of its major American Indian groups. Selected sites of interest are also shown (▲).

HOPI

ZUNI

NAVAJO

JICARILLA APACHE

Albuquerque

WESTERN APACHE

YAVAPAI

Colorado River

Phoenix

Gila

River

CHIRICAHUA APACHE

MESCALERO APACHE

PAPAGO AND UPPER PIMA

UNITED STATES

MEXICO

BAJA

CALIFORNIA

Gulf of California

OPATA

SUMA

Rio Grande

SOUTHWEST

UNITED STATES

MEXICO

Houston

LOWER PIMA

TARAHUMARA

CONCHO

SIERRA

MAYO

SIERRA

TOBOSCO

MADRE

Terreón

Monterrey

TEPEHUAN

MADRE

Mazatlán

ZACATEC

Guadalajara

The Jicarilla and Western Apache farmed extensively, while the Lipan and Mescalero Apache were bison hunters influenced by the nearby Plains Indians. The Chiricahua Apache, however, were much more aggressive than these other bands. From mountain strongholds they launched raids into New Mexico, Arizona, and northern Mexico.

Most Apaches never did settle and become farmers like other American Indians in the Southwest. Here a group of young Apache men pose with an Apache weapon: the bow and arrow.

Although the Navajo adopted farming techniques after contact with the Hopi in the 1700s and began raising corn, beans, squash, and melons, they too raided other tribes and European settlements. The Navajo lived in *hogans*, cone-shaped frameworks covered with bark and earth. Today, the Navajo represent the largest group of Native Americans in the United States.

The Hopi, in contrast, were a peaceful people. Like the Zuni, the Hopi are thought to be the descendants of the earlier Anasazi and Mogollon peoples, although their origins remain unclear. Like the Anasazi, the Hopi built multistory *pueblos* from logs and bricks of sun-dried mud (*adobe*), and towns were usually placed atop high mesas. Village centers usually held *kivas*, special ceremonial rooms dug into the ground.

Corn was by far the most important food to these desert farmers, but they also grew a variety of fruits and vegetables. The success of Hopi farming is all the more remarkable in the hot, dry climate of the Southwest. Crops were planted near underground springs or at the base of the mesas, where they could catch the runoff from any rainfall. The Hopi also herded sheep and kept flocks of turkeys for meat.

Kachinas, supernatural beings believed to live in the San Francisco Mountains, played an important part in Hopi religion. Men wore kachina masks and were embodiments of these spirits during ceremonies. Hopi parents carved kachina dolls representing the spirits and gave the dolls to their children.

Hopi kachinas are shown here in their human form. Part of their role during such ceremonies as this was to frighten Hopi children. Other members of the group watch from atop pueblos.

These young Apaches were photographed playing a game in Arizona in 1899. Apaches lived in many different bands, who had different life-styles but who all spoke the same language.

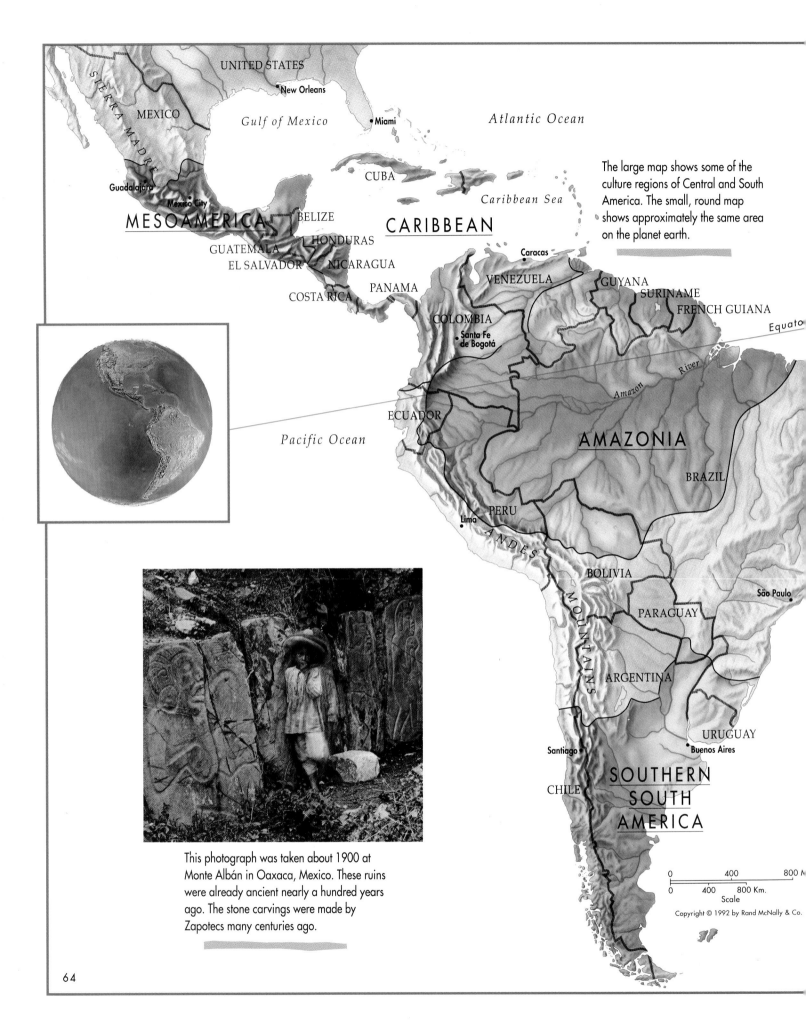

UNITED STATES

New Orleans

Gulf of Mexico

Miami

Atlantic Ocean

CUBA

MEXICO

SIERRA MADRE

Guadalajara

Mexico City

MESOAMERICA

BELIZE

CARIBBEAN

Caribbean Sea

GUATEMALA

HONDURAS

EL SALVADOR   NICARAGUA

COSTA RICA   PANAMA

Caracas

VENEZUELA

GUYANA

SURINAME

FRENCH GUIANA

COLOMBIA

Santa Fe
de Bogotá

Equato

Amazon River

The large map shows some of the
culture regions of Central and South
America. The small, round map
shows approximately the same area
on the planet earth.

ECUADOR

Pacific Ocean

AMAZONIA

BRAZIL

PERU

Lima

A N D E S

BOLIVIA

São Paulo

PARAGUAY

M O U N T A I N S

ARGENTINA

URUGUAY

Santiago

Buenos Aires

SOUTHERN
SOUTH
AMERICA

CHILE

This photograph was taken about 1900 at
Monte Albán in Oaxaca, Mexico. These ruins
were already ancient nearly a hundred years
ago. The stone carvings were made by
Zapotecs many centuries ago.

0   400   800 M

0   400   800 Km.
Scale

Copyright © 1992 by Rand McNally & Co.

64

CENTRAL AND SOUTH AMERICAN PEOPLES

ZAPOTEC

Ancestors of modern Zapotec lived in what is now southern Mexico. They created one of the early civilizations of ancient Mexico, predating both the Aztec and the Maya cultures. The Zapotec now live in the Mexican state of Oaxaca, and their beautiful weaving and distinctive sculpture are highly regarded. Today, over four hundred thousand people speak dialects of the Zapotec language.

By about 500 BC, the Zapotec were already successful farmers and city-dwellers. Their mountaintop ceremonial center of Monte Albán was located close to present-day Oaxaca City. It was here that scholars found the oldest dated *hieroglyphic*, or picture-based, records discovered in the Americas. Many of these suggest that military conquest was very important. The Zapotec also built an astronomical observatory at Monte Albán, and the development of the calendar that the Maya later made so precise probably began here.

Zapotec women and children pose here in Oaxaca around 1900. Zapotecs have inhabited this part of what is now Mexico for about two thousand years.

Between AD 300 and 900, Monte Albán supported a population of more than sixty thousand. The city held stone pyramids, palaces, and painted tombs, and the mountainside was terraced so that houses could be built there. The Zapotec were in part influenced by an even older culture to the north—the Olmec. Although the city was never completely abandoned, Monte Albán declined in importance after AD 800, and the Zapotec culture thrived in small towns. Another Native American group, the Mixtecs, invaded the cities along with most of the Valley of Oaxaca around 1300, forcing the Zapotec southward. The valley eventually became part of the expanding Aztec empire, but the southern Zapotec, who founded another ceremonial center at Mitla, maintained their independence until the arrival of Europeans.

66

UNITED STATES

MS AL
TX
LA

Gulf of Mexico

SIERRA MADRE

MEXICO

Shown here are the Mesoamerican and Caribbean culture areas and some of their major Native American groups. The enlarged map at upper right shows the Bahamas and the route Columbus took through them in 1492.

COLOTLAN

HUASTEC

Guadalajara

TOLTEC

TARASCAN

TOTONAC

Mexico City

MESOAMERICA

MAYA

MIXTEC

OLMEC

ZAPOTEC

MONTE ALBÁN   MITLA

BELIZE

MAYA

HONDUR

GUATEMALA

EL SALVADOR

NICARAG

ARAWAK

The Arawak inhabited the tropical forests of South America, especially north of the Amazon, extending from the foothills of the Andes Mountains to the chain of Caribbean islands that arc from South America to Florida. Now living mainly in the forests of northeastern Brazil, they farm, hunt, and fish the rivers.

The Arawak live in groups of fewer than two hundred people. Often, their settlements consist of a single building in which everyone lives. Before European contact, the Arawak along the coasts of present-day Guyana, Suriname, and Brazil gathered in much larger communities of more than one thousand people.

One Arawak group migrated northward from their South American homeland, settling throughout the islands of the Caribbean. These island Arawak called themselves the Taino. The Taino made good use of the rich resources of the islands.

The Taino gathered edible plants, hunted small animals, and fished the coastal waters in dugout canoes. They traveled as far away as Mexico and Florida, trading goods with the tribes who lived there. Both the Taino and their mainland relatives were peaceful farmers.

In the years before the arrival of Christopher Columbus, the fierce Carib Indians began a northern migration, driving the Arawak from the easternmost islands. In October 1492, with the arrival of Columbus in the Bahama Islands, the Taino became the first Native Americans the Europeans encountered. Because Columbus thought he had reached islands east of India, he called these people "Indians."

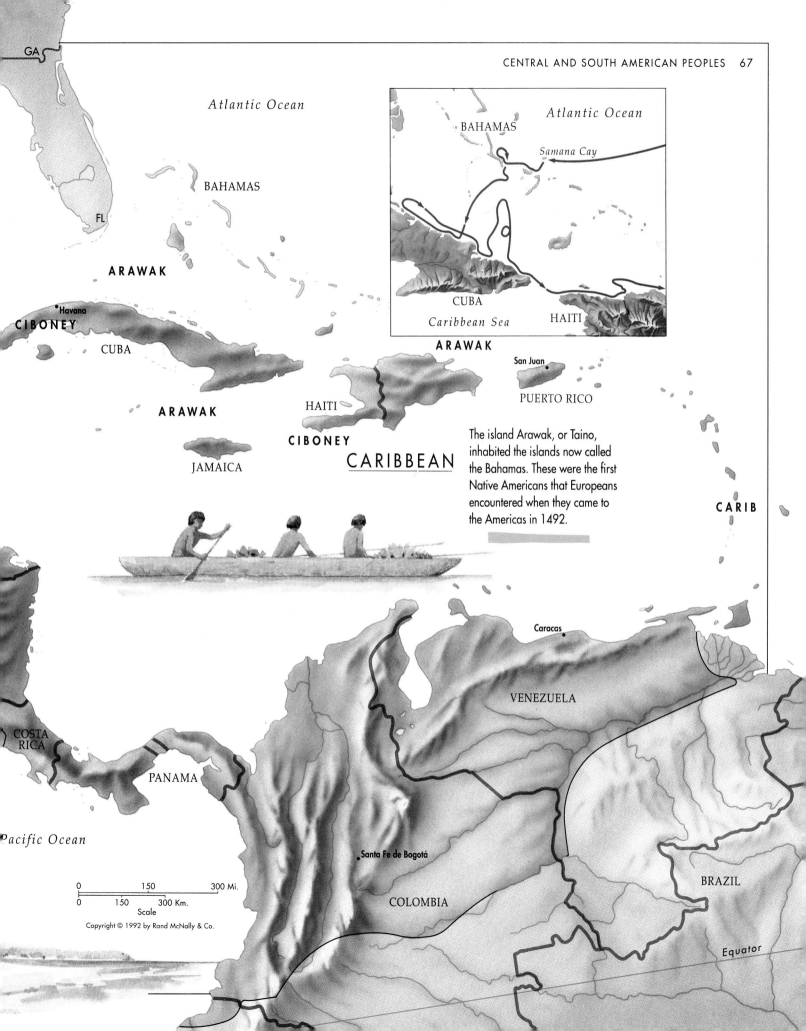

GA

Atlantic Ocean

BAHAMAS

FL

ARAWAK

•Havana

CIBONEY

CUBA

ARAWAK

JAMAICA

HAITI

CIBONEY

CARIBBEAN

Atlantic Ocean

BAHAMAS

Samana Cay

CUBA

Caribbean Sea

HAITI

ARAWAK

San Juan •

PUERTO RICO

The island Arawak, or Taino, inhabited the islands now called the Bahamas. These were the first Native Americans that Europeans encountered when they came to the Americas in 1492.

CARIB

Caracas •

VENEZUELA

COSTA
RICA

PANAMA

Pacific Ocean

0   150   300 Mi.
0   150   300 Km.
Scale

Santa Fe de Bogotá •

COLOMBIA

BRAZIL

Equator

Copyright © 1992 by Rand McNally & Co.

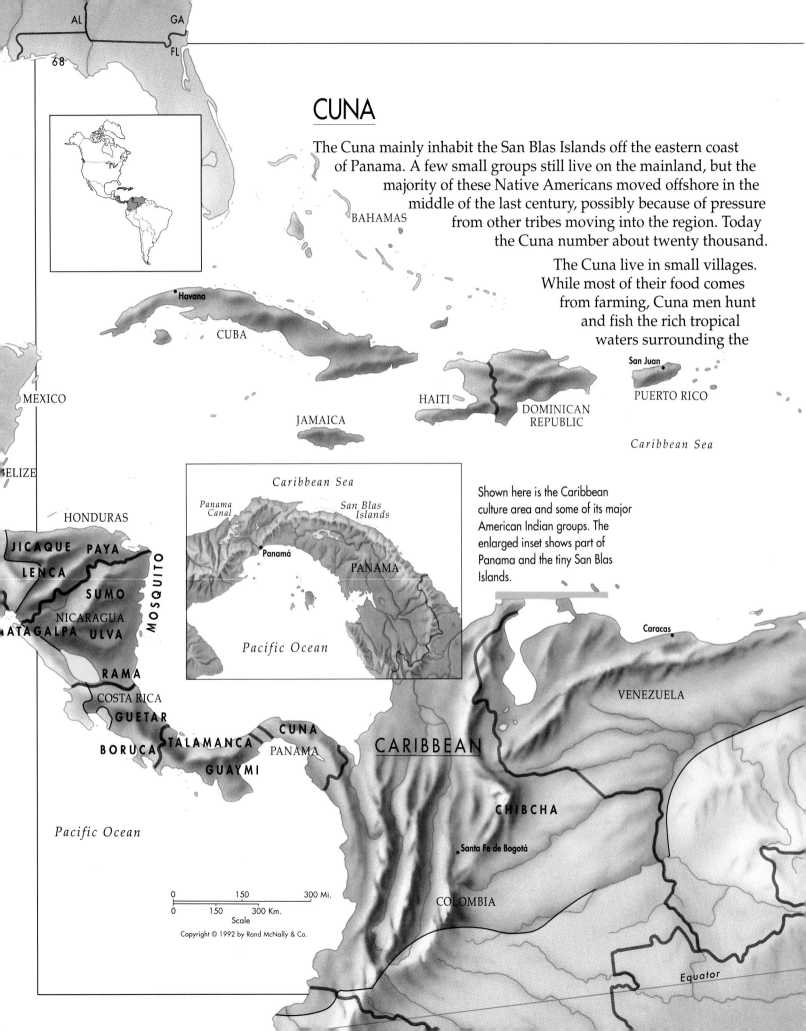

CUNA

The Cuna mainly inhabit the San Blas Islands off the eastern coast of Panama. A few small groups still live on the mainland, but the majority of these Native Americans moved offshore in the middle of the last century, possibly because of pressure from other tribes moving into the region. Today the Cuna number about twenty thousand.

The Cuna live in small villages. While most of their food comes from farming, Cuna men hunt and fish the rich tropical waters surrounding the

Shown here is the Caribbean culture area and some of its major American Indian groups. The enlarged inset shows part of Panama and the tiny San Blas Islands.

AL
GA
FL

BAHAMAS

Havana

CUBA

MEXICO

JAMAICA

HAITI

DOMINICAN REPUBLIC

San Juan

PUERTO RICO

Caribbean Sea

BELIZE

HONDURAS

JICAQUE   PAYA

LENCA

SUMO

NICARAGUA

MATAGALPA   ULVA

MOSQUITO

RAMA

COSTA RICA

GUETAR

BORUCA   TALAMANCA   CUNA

GUAYMI   PANAMA

Pacific Ocean

Caribbean Sea

Panama Canal

San Blas Islands

Panamá

PANAMA

Pacific Ocean

CARIBBEAN

Caracas

VENEZUELA

CHIBCHA

Santa Fe de Bogotá

COLOMBIA

Equator

0   150   300 Mi.
0   150   300 Km.
Scale

Copyright © 1992 by Rand McNally & Co.

islands. In fact the native word *Panama* means "an abundance of fish." Corn, beans, squash, rice, and citrus fruits are their most important agricultural products.

In Cuna religion, the souls of the dead must pass through eight layers of an underworld and then eight layers of heaven. *Shamans*, or spiritual guides, lead the souls on their complex journey through the layers of afterlife.

Like the Lenca Indians, who live to the north in an isolated part of Honduras, the Cuna still speak the language of the Chibcha. The Chibcha were farmers and built up a society nearly as complex as the Inca civilization in Peru. In the century before the arrival of Europeans, the Chibcha spread throughout present-day Colombia, living in permanent settlements of several thousand people. The capital city of modern Colombia, Bogotá, was the site of the main Chibcha ceremonial center.

The Chibcha divided their territory into five states, each of which was ruled by a single powerful chief. In the 1530s, when the Spanish began their conquest of the region, these states failed to unite against the invaders. The Chibcha, like the Inca, were defeated.

Atlantic Ocean

Cuna farmers grow most of the food they need, and the Caribbean waters provide them with plentiful fish. The reverse-appliqué blouses made by Cuna women—*molas*—are known throughout the world.

GUYANA

SURINAME

BRAZIL

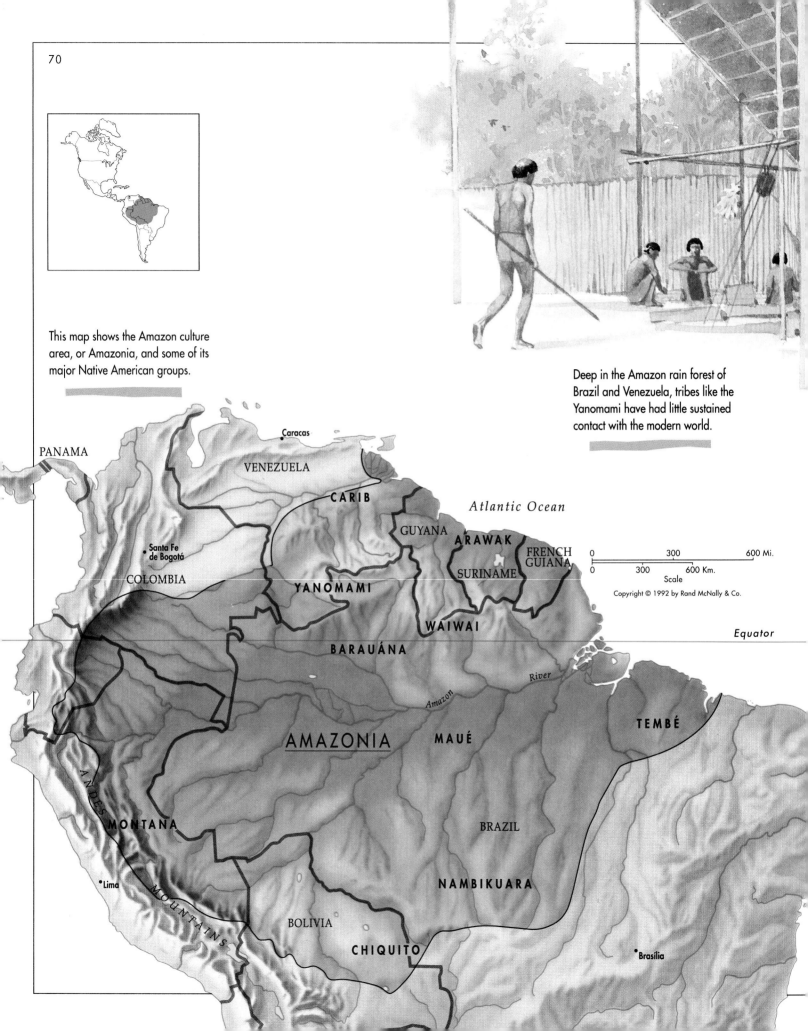

This map shows the Amazon culture area, or Amazonia, and some of its major Native American groups.

Deep in the Amazon rain forest of Brazil and Venezuela, tribes like the Yanomami have had little sustained contact with the modern world.

PANAMA

Caracas

VENEZUELA

CARIB

Atlantic Ocean

GUYANA

ARAWAK

FRENCH GUIANA

SURINAME

Santa Fe de Bogotá

0   300   600 Mi.

0   300   600 Km.
Scale

Copyright © 1992 by Rand McNally & Co.

COLOMBIA

YANOMAMI

WAIWAI

BARAUÁNA

Equator

Amazon

River

TEMBÉ

AMAZONIA

MAUÉ

ANDES

MONTANA

BRAZIL

Lima

NAMBIKUARA

MOUNTAINS

BOLIVIA

CHIQUITO

Brasília

YANOMAMI

Although Native Americans have occupied South America for at least ten thousand years, no one knows how long Indians have lived in the lush rain forest of the Amazon River basin. Hundreds of groups live here, and while they differ from one another in many ways, their life-styles have several features in common. They live in small communities, and most groups obtain food by hunting, fishing, and gathering plants, depending on the season. Few nonnatives have ventured deep into the Amazon until the last half of this century, so the Indians of the rain forest have had little sustained contact with outsiders.

The Yanomami is the largest tribe in the Americas still living in its primitive state. They live deep in the forest in northwestern Brazil and southern Venezuela. In 1991 both countries established protected areas of more than 30,000 square miles (78,000 square kilometers) for the undisturbed use of the Yanomami.

The tribe's language does not seem to be related to the languages spoken by any other South American group. The Yanomami had little contact with outsiders until the 1950s, and estimates of their number differ greatly—from ten thousand to forty thousand. Yanomami men frequently fight one another, and villages break up when blood relatives become enemies. Neighboring villages will often carry out raids against one another. For this reason, enemy villages are so widely separated that it may take several days to walk between them. However, villages on friendly terms may lie within just a few hundred feet of one another.

The Yanomami raise bananas and plantains, and they also gather palm fruit and hunt for additional food.

Mapuche women weave fabrics
on a Chilean reservation.

MAPUCHE

The Araucanians are a group
of Indians speaking related
languages who live in the
Andes Mountains of southern
South America. They were
once a widespread group of
farmers and herders, but their numbers
have decreased. The Mapuche, who live in the central valley of
Chile, represent the largest group of the Araucanian-speaking people.

Since the end of the last century, the Mapuche have lived on
reservations established by the Chilean government. About three
hundred thousand Mapuche live on these reservations today, making
them the largest Native American group in modern South America.
Those not living on the reservations have taken jobs in the cities of
Chile and Argentina.

The Mapuche resisted the southward push of the great Inca empire.
Additionally, they are famous for their three-century-long struggle
with the Spanish and, later, Chilean armies. These conflicts forced them
to reorganize their traditional life-style. Distant villages formed military
and political alliances, and Mapuche warriors learned to use horses.

Farming remains the main activity of the Mapuche, and crops
include corn, potatoes, beans, squash, chili peppers, and other
vegetables. In the past, women usually cared for the crops while the
men fought battles with other Mapuche groups or with the Spanish.
Today, though, men usually work the farms while the women cultivate
smaller vegetable gardens. Fishing and hunting were also important
to the Mapuche's ancient way of life. They kept llamas for carrying
goods, and at one time a man's wealth was determined by the number
of llamas he owned. Today, however, the llama herds have been
replaced by horses, sheep, cattle, and other livestock.

PERU

BRAZIL

BOLIVIA

Pacific Ocean

PARAGUAY

GUARANÍ

CHILE

URUGUAY

COMECHINGON

CHARRÚA

Santiago

HUARPE

QUERANDÍ

Buenos Aires

OICO

ARGENTINA

SOUTHERN SOUTH AMERICA

This map shows the Southern South American culture area and some of its major American Indian groups.

CHECHEHET

MAPUCHE

PUELCHE

The Mapuche belong to a larger group known as Araucanians. This scene shows two Araucanian medicine women, or shamans, at work in about 1920.

CHONO   TEHUELCHE

Atlantic Ocean

ALACALUF

ONA

YAHGAN

0   300   600 Mi.

0   300   600 Km.

Scale

Copyright © 1992 by Rand McNally & Co.

GLOSSARY

adobe A brick made from sun-dried mud and straw and used by Southwest Indians to make pueblos.

aqueduct A conduit for bringing fresh drinking water from distant sources into cities.

asphalt A thick, dark-colored liquid formed in oil-bearing rocks; also called *tar* or *pitch*. The Chumash used asphalt to make their plank boats watertight.

barabaras A large Aleut dwelling built from driftwood, whale bone, and sod.

bas-relief A type of sculpture that rises very little from the background; low relief. Typical of many groups in Mesoamerica.

Bering Land Bridge Land connecting Asia and North America that emerged during the last Ice Age, when the sea level was much lower than today. The first humans reached North America by this route.

buffalo A hoofed mammal with a dark-brown coat, shaggy mane, and short curved horns. They were an essential resource of the Plains Indians. Also called *bison*.

bullboat A circular, cup-shaped boat made from hide stretched over a wooden frame. Typical of the Mandan and other Indians along the upper Missouri River.

caribou A deer found in the Arctic and Subarctic regions of North America.

confederacy A political union of several tribes.

coup stick A special stick often used in battle to harmlessly touch an enemy, although the side of a weapon or even the warrior's hand were also used. Among Plains Indians this was done to prove bravery.

culture area A geographical region where different Indian tribes had similar languages and life-styles.

dugout A type of boat made by hollowing out a log.

earth lodge A large, usually dome-shaped dwelling made by covering a log frame with plant material, then packed with mud.

earthwork Any large earthen structure made by ancient Indians for burials, to represent animals or special symbols, or to hold temples or houses. Such "mound building" cultures were widespread in the eastern half of North America.

glacier A large mass of ice formed on land by the compaction of snow that creeps forward due to the force of its own weight. Ice sheets and glaciers covered much of North America during periods called Ice Ages.

gourd The dried and hollowed-out shell of fruits with hard, durable rinds used as tools or ornaments. They are part of the same vine family that produces pumpkin, squash, and cucumber.

hammock A hanging cot suspended between two supports made from cotton netting and used by the Taino of the Caribbean.

hieroglyphic A system of writing using pictures instead of letters. Developed to a high degree by Mesoamerican cultures, particularly the Maya.

hogan A Navajo dwelling with a log and stick frame usually covered with mud or sod.

Ice Age One of many periods in Earth's history during which glaciers and ice sheets advanced across the continents. The last Ice Age reached its peak about 20,000 years ago.

igloo A dome-shaped temporary dwelling made from blocks of ice; also called a *snow house*. The Central Eskimo lived in igloos during the winter.

Kachina A supernatural being in the religion of the Hopis, Zunis, and other Pueblo Indians. Kachina masks are worn in tribal ceremonies to impersonate these beings, and kachina dolls are given to children for study.

kayak A one- or two-man boat used by Eskimos and made by stretching hide over a wooden frame.

kiva An underground ceremonial chamber typical of the Anasazi and Hopi Indians.

longhouse An Iroquois dwelling with a rounded roof and doors at both ends, made with a pole frame and usually covered with elm bark. Usually ten Iroquois families lived in each longhouse.

mesa A flat-topped elevation with steep sides found in the Southwest. The Anasazi built their villages atop mesas.

nomad A way of life in which people frequently moved from one location to another in search of food.

permafrost A layer of permanently frozen soil, typical of Arctic lands.

pit house A dwelling formed by placing a log frame covered with mud or plant materials over a hole.

plantain A large tropical plant that bears fruit similar to bananas.

potlatch An extravagant tribal ceremony of during which possessions are given away to demonstrate wealth. Typical of Northwest Coast Indians.

pueblo A type of dwelling common among Southwest Indians. Made from stone or adobe bricks, they can be five stories high and contain many apartment-like rooms. Ladders are used to move between different levels.

quipu A counting aid made of knotted strings used by the Incas of South America.

reservation A tract of land set aside by the government for use by Indians.

shaman A member of a tribe who interprets and attempts to control the supernatural.

snowshoe A device for walking on top of deep snow, made from a wooden frame laced with leather webbing.

tepee (or tipi) A conical tent with a pole frame and usually covered with buffalo hides. Typical of the Plains Indians.

totem pole A post carved and painted with a series of figures and symbols, of special meaning with regard to tribal legends and history. Typical of Northwest Coast Indians.

Trail of Tears The Cherokee term for the harsh journey to Indian Territory (now Oklahoma) when the U.S. Government forced them from their native lands in the 1830s, along with the Choctaw, Creek, Chickasaw, Seminole.

umiak A large, open, flat-bottomed boat made by stretching an animal hide over a wooden frame. Typical of the Eskimos.

wickiup A cone-shaped or domed dwelling with a pole frame covered with brush, grass, or reeds. Typical of the Apaches in the Southwest and some Great Basin tribes.

wigwam A domed or cone-shaped dwelling with a pole frame covered with bark, animal skin, or mats of woven plant matter. Typical of many Subarctic and Northeast tribes.

wild rice Actually a grass with an edible grain, this tall plant grows along the western Great Lakes. It was an important food source for the Indians of this region.

Xingu Park A protected area in central Brazil founded in 1961. Native groups whose way of life was threatened by development of the rain forest were brought here.

INDEX

PEOPLING THE PLANET

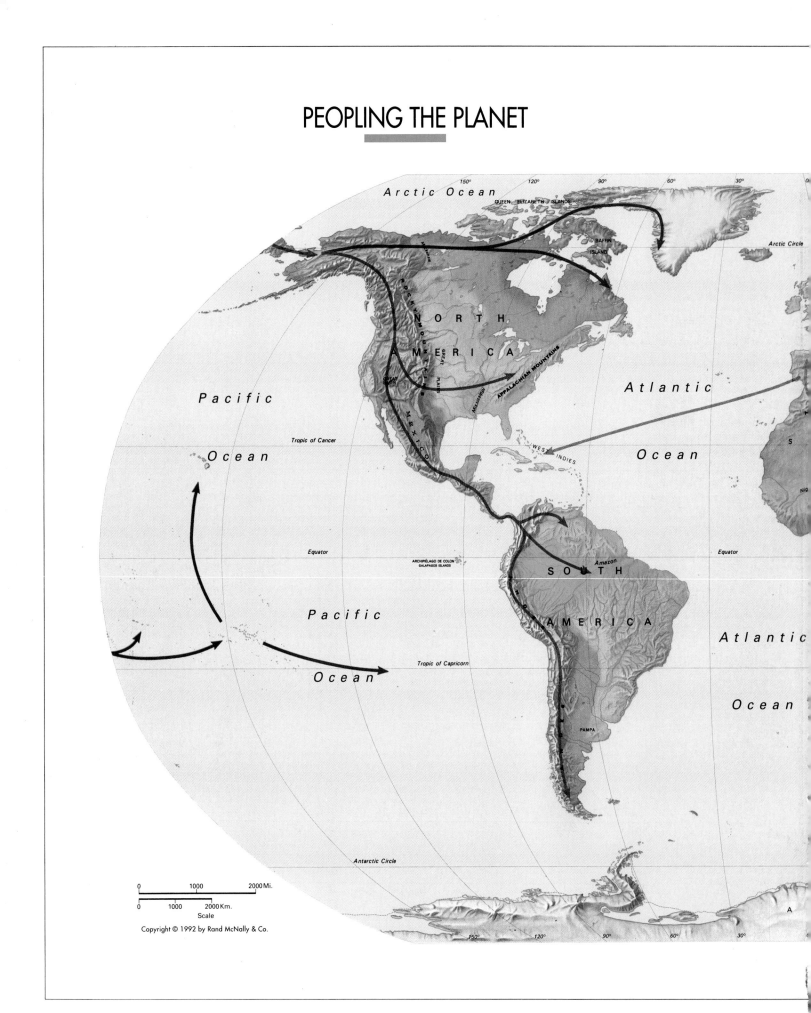